JUDGEMENT AT STONEY CREEK

JUDGEMENT AT STONEY CREEK

BRIDGET MORAN

ARSENAL PULP PRESS
Vancouver

JUDGEMENT AT STONEY CREEK
Copyright © 1990 Bridget Moran
Preface to new edition © 1998 Bridget Moran

THIRD PRINTING: 1998

Originally published by Tillacum Library, an imprint of Arsenal Pulp Press.

ARSENAL PULP PRESS
103-1014 Homer Street
Vancouver, B.C.
Canada v6b 2w9

The publisher gratefully acknowledges the support of the Canada Council for the Arts for its publishing program, and the support of the Book Publishing Industry Development Program, and the B.C. Arts Council.

Typeset by the Vancouver Desktop Publishing Centre
Cover photo courtesy of the Vancouver Public Library (#33579)
Printed and bound in Canada

CANADIAN CATALOGUING IN PUBLICATION DATA:
Moran, Bridget, 1923-
  Judgement at Stoney Creek

  ISBN 1-55152-053-2

  1. Thomas, Coreen. 2. Redekop, Richard—Trials, litigation, etc. 3. Trials (Negligence, Criminal)—British Columbia—Vanderhoof. 4. Discrimination in criminal justice administration—British Columbia. I. Title.
KE229.R44M67 1998   345.711'05'08997   C98-910076-6
KF224.R44M67 1998

Acknowledgements

I wish to express my thanks to the people of Stoney Creek, especially the Thomas family.

I also wish to express my gratitude to Harry Rankin, to the Canada Council, to Randy Fred, Brian Lam, and Linda Field of Arsenal Pulp Press/Tillacum Library, and last but not least, to my agent who is also my daughter, Roseanne Moran.

Preface to the New Edition

ON SEPTEMBER 24, 1997—the twenty-first anniversary of the inquest into the death of Coreen Thomas—I made one of my frequent visits to Stoney Creek Reserve, nine miles south of Vanderhoof. As I followed Highway 16 through the town, turned left at the sign pointing to the reserve, and ascended the steep hill approaching 6th Street, I remembered—as I always do at that intersection—the tragic death of Coreen and her unborn baby. And I suddenly realized that if Coreen had not been hit by a car driven by Richard Redekop in the early hours of July 2, 1976, she would now be forty-two years old, and the baby boy who died with her would be twenty-one.

As I continued the drive to Stoney Creek, I recalled the media stories, the letters to the editor, the numerous reporters, and the grief and anger that followed Coreen's death. For me, those tumultuous months will always be associated with her name, her brief life. The people of Stoney Creek remember her too; they have not forgotten the struggle, led by Coreen's aunt Sophie Thomas, to force an inquest into her death. For them, it was an unsettling and confusing time. Unused to the harsh glare of publicity, they found themselves awash in a flood of newspaper headlines: INDIANS HARASSED ON ROAD; RACISM AND BRUTALITY RAMPANT; VANDERHOOF CORONER WITHDRAWS FROM INQUEST; WITNESS ACCUSES CONSTABLE OF FORCING HER TO LIE; CONSTABLE DENIES MAKING GIRL LIE; RICHARD REDEKOP NEGLIGENT; and finally, in June 1977, REDEKOP ACQUITTED OF ROAD DEATH.

Charges of racism ran like an ugly fault line through those

7

months. Twenty-one years later, I am routinely asked: "What about racism now? Does "Two Solitudes" still describe the relationship between Vanderhoof and Stoney Creek?" The Native students who attend school in Vanderhoof, the Natives who apply for jobs in stores or other places of business in the town, the Carrier elders who spend money—a good deal of money—in its mall and then are told to keep moving when they stop for a chat—these people from Stoney Creek would answer, yes, racism is still a fact of life for them.

Perhaps the most bitter fact of all for band members is that the town's racism is expressed in blatant economic terms: despite the hundreds of thousands of dollars Stoney Creek Natives spend each month in Vanderhoof's places of business, these same shops and outlets almost never employ Aboriginals.

If this economic racism and social separation existed only in Vanderhoof, if the months of nation-wide publicity exposing the two solitudes at the time of Coreen Thomas' death had resulted in a more tolerant and accepting Canada, the people of Stoney Creek would feel there had been some recompense for their struggle with the justice system. Sad to say, this is not the case. Stoney Creek is merely a microcosm reflecting a Canada where Aboriginals still live with the reality of racism, and one of its most vicious first fruits, unemployment.

But Natives have proven that despite all odds, they are survivors. They have learned, usually the hard way, that in Canada they must depend on themselves, especially in the field of employment. If the wider community will not hire them, they will create work in their own territory. Nowhere is this more true than in Stoney Creek. Thanks to the monumental efforts of the band, especially the elders, twelve men from the reserve now work in the bush for Neduchen (Our Wood) managing a tree license, and seventy-five men and women are employed in Dezti Wood, a joint venture involving three reserves to process value-added wood. Elders will say that it took twenty years of struggle with the Department of Indian Affairs to get these economic projects in place, "but at least," they say, "we have them now."

Some things have changed for the better—Natives can now enter restaurants, bars, and hotels, and the hospital no longer has its "Indian wing"—but in less obvious ways, the separation of Natives and non-Natives is still a fact of life in the Nechako Valley. Despite the reality of this separation, however, Stoney Creek is no longer the impoverished reserve it was in 1976. At the time of Coreen's death it was one of the poorest reservations in British Columbia—its statistics for unemployment, inadequate housing and living conditions, violence, and alcohol abuse were among the highest in the province. There were no sewage or water systems. Incidents of tuberculosis were increasing. The gravel road running through the reserve to Kenny Dam enveloped the reserve in a cloud of dust for much of the year, and was the subject of more than one biting comment from lawyer Harry Rankin, acting for the Indian Homemakers Association during the inquest.

Twenty-one years later, the population is growing; there is much new housing; streetlights and water and sewage systems are in place. Thanks to a blockade set up by the band, the road through the reserve is now paved. The Elder Society is strong and actively involved in cultural, spiritual, and economic reserve life. An Elders project, the Potlatch House, is much in demand as a conference centre, and since it was completed in the 1980s, has hosted a number of Carrier assemblies, potlatches, feasts, and special events. Stoney Creek village now has a hostel for single men, a learning centre for upgrading education, a large multiplex built by the band, and a new church. A health clinic and school are also in the building stage.

Like other reservations in Canada, substance abuse, violence, and pockets of poverty and unemployment still plague the band, but despite the reality of these social ills, Stoney Creek today is a far cry from the desolate community of two decades ago.

SO MANY OF THE PEOPLE who became familiar to reporters during the months leading up to Rick Redekop's trial have passed away: Coroner Eric Turner, Coroner Glen MacDonald, Coreen's mother Matilda, the husbands of Elders Mary John and Sophie Thomas, Mary John's daughter Helen and her husband Don, Dr. Charles Stephen, that flamboyant witness Cecil Raphael, and tearful Faye Haugen, to name just a few.

Many others flourish and some of them continue to make headlines: Harry Rankin, now seventy-seven, still enlivens the halls of justice. Cliff Macarthur eventually went on to a judgeship. In October 1997, Bishop Remi De Roo celebrated thirty-five years as Bishop of the Victoria Diocese. Sid (now Syd) Simons continues to practice criminal law in Victoria, and Bruce Allan, fifteen years old when he witnessed Coreen's death, has a master's degree and teaches Native Studies in the college and university systems. Archie Patrick is band manager of a reservation in the B.C. Lower Mainland. Geraldine Thomas, whose poem "Roads of My People" was written at age twelve in 1976, has completed years of post-secondary education and now works for the Stoney Creek Band. Ken Luggi, foreman of the inquest jury, continues to provide guidance and support for his people. Coreen's father Peter, a respected elder, and his daughter Margie, now in her mid-thirties, live in Stoney Creek. Rick Redekop with his second wife moved to the Okanagan Valley.

And what of Sophie Thomas?

Now in her late seventies, Sophie is still the activist she always was. Perhaps today she is best known for her dedication to the environment and her knowledge and use of Native medicines. Her wisdom is much in demand in colleges, universities, in environmental and forestry conferences, and on television, as she speaks for the healing and sustaining powers of the rivers and lakes, the trees, shrubs, plants, and berries. She constantly shares her curative knowledge of Native medicine with people throughout the province.

THE QUESTION CAN BE ASKED: with all the sound and fury of those months in 1976 and 1977, was the cause of justice served? Probably the jury is still out on that one.

Nonetheless, Sophie Thomas' cry for justice, and the activist efforts of the band which supported her, changed Stoney Creek forever. During this time, band members became politicized—they discovered that in unity there was power, and when they took that power into their own hands, change was possible. Improvements have been slow in coming, and often not without a struggle, but come they have.

Perhaps that is the final Judgement at Stoney Creek.

—BRIDGET MORAN
Prince George, B.C.
March 1998

Roads of My People

There are roads, roads of my people,
I hear footsteps upon the dense gravel.
Looking against the dim shade of the dawn sky
I see the figure of a woman . . .
A native woman.
Pregnant she was, yet she carried on.
But where? . . .
To the destiny of her people.

Voices of one's friends broke the silence
Like water trickling over the rocky bottom of a small creek below.

Suddenly I see a moving light, followed by an innocent scream
. . . that ended in darkness.

The warm winds blew over, taking away that last breath of life.

There are roads, roads of my people.
Grim faces, I say,
But injustice will never pay.

My brother, I call him . . . betrayed me.

—GERALDINE THOMAS,
Coreen's twelve-year-old cousin, Fall of 1976

Introduction

A S CANADA MOVED INTO THE 1990s, we could look back on the past decade as a time when more than one judicial inquiry probed the relationship between aboriginal people and the country's justice system. At the very least these inquiries served to confirm what many of us already knew—that in this country, liberty, even life, can be endangered through the simple fact of being born an Indian.

During one of these judicial inquiries we heard of a young Native lad, Donald Marshall, imprisoned in Nova Scotia for more than a decade for a murder he did not commit. From the evidence presented it is difficult to escape the conclusion that he went from the dock to prison because he was a Micmac, and that his story would have been very different if he had been white. In fact, the report of the inquiry released in January 1990 stated unequivocally that Donald Marshall spent those eleven years behind bars because the white justice system, with its lethal mixture of incompetence and racism, failed him at every turn. The Province of Nova Scotia and the RCMP have since apologized to him for 'mistakes' of the past, and have promised to mend their ways. Unfortunately such abject apologies do little to compensate Donald Marshall for what he describes as the empty spot there will always be in his life.

We heard of a Native leader J.J. (John Joseph) Harper, accosted and killed by the police on a street in Winnipeg. Evidence seemed to indicate that the policemen, chasing a fugitive, an Indian running from a stolen car, lost the original culprit and targeted the first Native who appeared on the street—it was J.J. Harper's ill luck to be that Native. The proceedings of the Manitoba judicial inquiry into his death heard incredible tales of forged documents, doctored statements, missing evidence. Much of the testimony disclosed a concerted effort on the part of the police department to make J.J. Harper responsible for his own death or, failing this, to make his death look like a regrettable accident.

And we shuddered as we heard details of the tragic case of Helen Betty Osborne, age nineteen and a Cree, stabbed fifty-six times with a screwdriver because she would not have sex with four drunken white men. Was it because she was an Indian that sixteen years elapsed before anyone was charged with her murder? For years all sorts of people, including justice personnel in the town of The Pas, Manitoba, appear to have known the names of the four men who forced Helen Betty Osborne into the car on that fatal night. For sixteen years those four men walked the streets of Canadian towns and cities as free and, in some cases, respected citizens. To this day only one of the four men has been found guilty as charged and is serving time in prison.

Over and over again as I followed the reports of these judicial inquiries, the names Marshall, Harper, Osborne, were repeated and a thought, more than a thought, kept recurring. The names of Coreen Thomas and her baby, I was convinced, also belonged in that sad galaxy of Natives whom our justice system has failed.

THE BEGINNING FOR ME was deceptively simple—just a few lines in the local paper on a summer's day in 1976 announcing the death of a young Native girl. The name was Thomas, Coreen Thomas from Stoney Creek Indian Reservation.

The first newspaper article served to create the impression that Coreen had caused her own death. "The woman," said the report, "apparently darted in front of a car driven by Richard

Brian Redekop. . . . Police are continuing an investigation of the accident." From this report, one had a picture of a car proceeding in a normal way under normal conditions and of a young woman jeopardizing her own life by running in front of it.

My first thought on reading the account was that Coreen must have been a relative of Sophie Thomas, a respected elder from Stoney Creek Reserve. I had first visited Stoney Creek village as a provincial social worker in 1954, and in the years which followed that first visit, I had come to know Sophie. I had great affection for her and as I read, I sent a silent message of sympathy over the miles to her.

Before many days had elapsed, however, I realized that although sympathy was all very well, Sophie wanted something more, something else—she was in fact demanding action from the white justice system.

When I visited Stoney Creek a few days after Coreen's death, I heard stories which shattered that first impression of a senseless accident which I had gained from the original newspaper article. Stoney Creek youngsters said that the Redekop vehicle was travelling very fast when Coreen was struck and that the driver had been drinking. The noise and speed of the car and its bright headlights, said some of the witnesses, frightened Coreen and caused her to become disoriented. Some said that the ambulance had been too long in coming; others told me that Coreen had been within days of giving birth to a child and that no attempt had been made to save either her or the baby. With these and other rumours circulating, I learned that Sophie Thomas was asking for an inquest into Coreen's death. It soon became apparent that the local coroner and the RCMP had decided that an inquest was not necessary, and that a coroner's inquiry would meet the needs of the case.

No doubt the powers-that-be expected that the past would repeat itself one more time and that the Natives would talk of these rumours, these stories, only among themselves. Yes, they would talk—so must have run the expectation—but gradually the memory of Coreen's death would fade as the people of Stoney Creek took up the more urgent problems of day-to-day living. Another sad chapter would have been added to the sad history of a reservation, and that presumably would end the matter.

Imagine the shock then to any number of people both inside and outside the judicial system when there was a veritable torrent of words and charges which echoed far beyond the reserve's boundaries. Put simply, instead of sounds of silence, Sophie Thomas went public. She was not alone. In 1942 the women of Stoney Creek had become part of the British Columbia Homemakers Association, dedicated to improving their skills as wives and mothers. Before 1976 the Homemakers tended to leave Native politics to others—to the chief, the priest, or the Indian Agent. As pressure mounted for an inquest into Coreen's death, however, the Native Homemakers found that they were no longer content simply to knit and crochet and listen to talks about childcare from a social worker or a public health nurse. They moved into the political arena with Sophie and demanded an inquest into Coreen's death.

Elsewhere I describe the monumental struggle Sophie and her people waged to force an inquest. In fighting for that inquest they exposed the poverty, the unemployment, the poor living conditions which existed on their reserve. Through newspaper reports and in personal visits to Stoney Creek I became aware of another element in their struggle—I saw that the racism inherent in the Canadian justice system was also being exposed by the people of Stoney Creek.

When the inquest was finally ordered and when I heard that my old friend Harry Rankin was going to represent the British Columbia Indian Homemakers at that inquest, I phoned him at his law office in Vancouver. I reminded him that although I had been suspended (or as some say, defrocked!) by the governing Social Credit party in 1964 for my public criticisms of the welfare system, I had continued my contact with many people on Stoney Creek reserve.

What, I asked, did he know about Stoney Creek?

"I know plenty about reserves in general, but about that particular reserve, not a damn thing!" he replied.

"Right!" I said. "I will send you a sociological profile of the reserve—health, welfare, housing, employment—the works!"

And I did. I met with the chief, band councillors, elders—I questioned everyone who could help me to draw a realistic picture of life on Stoney Creek Reserve in the year 1976. My study went to Harry Rankin a few days before the inquest opened.

It goes without saying that I attended the inquest. I made repeated visits to Stoney Creek in the months which followed, and I attended the trial, nearly one year after Coreen's death, when Richard Redekop was acquitted of criminal negligence. When that trial was finally over I went to the pub with a group of young people, white and Native, and I listened as they voiced their anger, their frustration at the fact that, as they phrased it, "That bastard Redekop got away with it!"

In the pub and in the years since then my own frustration has been of a different sort; it was, and has continued to be, directed at the functioning of the justice system in its relation to the aboriginal people. It positively angered me that many people, both Native and white, had to exert so much pressure simply to ensure that an inquest would be held into the death of Coreen. Sophie Thomas said at the time, "If she had been a white girl, it would not have been like this," and I echoed her words. It frustrated me, as it frustrated the people of Stoney Creek that after the inquest, when they had every right to expect certain actions to follow, there was nothing. "It was like a big curtain came down between us and the white world again," said one elder.

I reached a conclusion about the reason for this inaction. I concluded that from the beginning the people in the justice system—police, coroner, crown counsel, and the rest—refused to deviate from the assumption that Coreen Thomas was the author of her own death. Further I concluded that this assumption was based, however vaguely, on a feeling that because Coreen was Indian she was probably drunk, and that it would not be unusual for a drunken Indian to run in front of a car. The coroner Eric Turner and the Vanderhoof RCMP made it clear from the start that they believed Coreen to be responsible for her own death. They held to this despite the fact that the inquest jurors, after hearing four days and two nights of evidence, attached no blame to Coreen, and instead ascribed responsibility to the driver of the car.

Following the inquest Crown Counsel's office in Prince George took no action. Finally the bereaved father of the girl took matters into his own hands and laid a charge of criminal negligence. Even then Crown Counsel A.S.K. Cook, having consulted with the Attorney General's Department in Victoria, said that the charge would not proceed because of insufficient evidence. It was only when this decision led to pressure from many groups that the Attorney General's office was forced to do an about-face. Finally it was announced that the charge would proceed. In the end, as events proved, the trial which followed in June 1977 merely confirmed the basic assumption that Coreen was the author of her own death.

"The judges and prosecutors attend [trials in Vanderhoof] from Prince George and Quesnel." So said an article on Page 6 of the *Vancouver Sun* dated December 6, 1976. This being the expected course, it seemed odd that this procedure was not followed in the 1977 trial of Richard Redekop. When it appeared that a charge of criminal negligence must proceed, a judge and a prosecutor from the Peace River country were appointed. I read of the appointments in the local paper a few days before Redekop was to be tried and I felt uneasy. The people of Stoney Creek were even more uneasy. As far as they were concerned, these purveyors of justice might as well have come from Borneo or Outer Mongolia. This judge, they asked each other, who is he? And the prosecutor, this man Clancey, will he be acting on our behalf, and if so, can someone tell us something about him? What does he know about us, they asked, and what does he know about Coreen's death?

Ironically the June 1977 trial seemed in keeping with the preceding events. As it was in the beginning, so it was at the end—Coreen was to be judged the author of her own death. In the words of the judge as he agreed to a dismissal of the charges against Richard Redekop, Coreen "made a grave error in judgement in leaving the hand of her sister and deciding to cross the road at a time when a vehicle was so close an accident was inevitable."

SOPHIE THOMAS SAID, "If Coreen had been white, things would have been different." One could as easily say, "If Donald Marshall—or J.J. Harper—or Helen Betty Osborne—had been white, things would have been different." The common denominator in all four cases is the presence of racism in the justice system. Without that virus the Coreen Thomas/Richard Redekop matter could have been regarded as an isolated incident. With it, Coreen and her baby join the list, longer than any of us will ever know, of Natives who were denied the protection of an impartial rule of law.

On September 27, 1976, the third night of the inquest into Coreen's death, a traditional meal was served to reporters, lawyers and friends in the home of elders Lazare and Mary John in Stoney Creek village. It was a balmy autumn night and in the living room after a dinner of roast moose and bannock and smoked salmon, there was talk of many things. In that flow of talk, lawyer Harry Rankin sounded a warning which lingered long after he had spoken. "If we don't come to terms with racism," he said slowly, "with the categorizing of some people as sub-humans, which is what racism is all about, maybe we won't survive at all."

In the hope of contributing something to that survival, and at the risk of opening old wounds, I wrote *Judgement at Stoney Creek*.

1

IF SOMEONE WERE SEEKING the exact centre of the province of British Columbia, it would be well to pinpoint Stoney Creek Indian Reservation. The reserve, or a spot a very few miles from it, is the central point in the province.

As a matter of fact it was a mandarin or two in far-off Ottawa who in the year 1870 looked at this central part of British Columbia and, with the instruments of the day, drew up boundaries for an Indian reservation. These same mandarins noted that a busy wandering creek ran through much of the reserve. One can imagine a couple of Anglo-Saxon gentlemen, complete with sideburns and polished boots, sitting in a panelled office in Ottawa and saying with a touch of surprise at their own originality, "Right! We'll name the reserve after that creek!" And no doubt, in some such way, with a local government agent and a priest or two explaining the boundaries to the Natives, Stoney Creek Indian Reservation was born. British Columbia was still a colony when the reservation of Stoney Creek was created; another year would elapse before this western territory joined confederation and henceforth bore the proud title of the province.

The elders on the reserve say that only after 1890 did the village of Stoney Creek, as distinct from the larger area of the reservation, come into being. "Long ago," said Adnas Alexis, "there was no village down here at Stoney Creek. Tatchik, down about a mile, Nulki, at the end of Nulki Lake, and Laketown, four miles up the lake—these were the only places people lived.

They lived in these places because of the fish. This was before 1890. All there was, was a trail going through where Stoney Creek village is now. One made a residing place just where the graveyard is now and from then on, people started moving into the village of Stoney Creek, one at a time. They all started moving in from Tatchik and Nulki Lake on account of the fish spawning up Stoney Creek. People were dependent for their livelihood on fish and that is why, you see, every Indian village is by a lake or a river or wherever there is fish."

By the time the twentieth century was a few years old, Stoney Creek was a settlement of nearly two hundred people, housed in rows of log buildings, living on game and fish and berries, enduring the dry heat of summer, the bitter cold of winter. There were months when the village was almost empty of people, for Stoney Creek Natives were nomadic, moving from the settlement to hunting grounds and traplines as season followed season.

Their wanderings in those years are remembered with nostalgia by the elders of today. "Even as children," says Mary John, a Stoney Creek great-grandmother, "we knew that the work at Stoney Creek in the summer, and the hunting and fishing in September in Cluculz Lake, meant food for the family. The trapline in winter was different. The skins we got there were sold, and it was this money which provided the family with clothing and flour and sugar and tea. Everything we did, the places in which we lived—all, all were important to the survival of the family. Even as a child, I understood that this was so."

NINE MILES AWAY, NORTH AND a bit east, at a swampy stretch in a bend of the Nechako River, two brothers, Ruben and Clarence Lampitt, trapped for marten. Neither the people of Stoney Creek, nor the Lampitt brothers for that matter, could have foreseen that within a few years, with a rumour running

wild that a railway was to be built through the territory, pros-
pectors and merchants and land developers from North America
and Europe would converge on this stretch of land beside the
river and carve out the townsite of Vanderhoof.

By 1920, although Stoney Creek village had a larger population than the townsite on the Nechako River, the sign of things
to come was there for all to see.

Stoney Creek had neither store nor school nor entrepreneur
of any kind. In contrast, in this same year Vanderhoof had a
doctor, a bank, drug and grocery and department stores, a
restaurant, a school, a fur dealer, a hotel, a notary public, a land
surveyor, a newspaper. A railway line skirted the settlement.
Already the people of the townsite were talking of incorporation
under the Village Municipalities Act. This in fact occurred in
1926, and the land along the bend of the Nechako River was
henceforth known as the Village of Vanderhoof.

The growth of the village reflected the times.

"The year just closed," wrote the editor of the local newspaper on January 6, 1934, "was not marked by outstanding events
and signs of great progress; but Vanderhoof was able to do what
many communities have not been able to do thus far in the
thirties—mark time—and keep its head above the water line. . . .
There have been few cases of real distress, so far as we know;
and most people have sufficient to live with some degree of
comfort." Not all reports in those years were as sanguine. In a
later edition of the paper, there is an account of a young widow
who supported her three children on a homestead during the
depression years. She borrowed a plow and a team of horses, in
return for which she dug potatoes and raked hay for a neighbour.
With the plow she cleared her land and put in vegetables and
hay. Her gun kept her children supplied with moose and bear
for food.

The 1940s saw a return to prosperity for Vanderhoof with a

post-war boom, intensified by the opening of the Consolidated Mining and Smelting Mercury Mine at Pinchi Lake, north of Vanderhoof. During the Second World War this mine supplied most of the mercury required by the Allies. The 1950s brought construction of the Kenney Dam, south of Vanderhoof; in the 1960s, Endako Mines, Canada's largest molydenum producer, the second largest in the world, began operations fifty miles west of the village of Vanderhoof.

These developments west, south, and north of Vanderhoof, together with a thriving lumber industry, assured the town a slow and steady growth. In 1976 Vanderhoof had a population of well over two thousand people, a deceptive figure since many more hundreds lived in the rich farming and ranching area which surrounds the town. When Vanderhoof celebrated the fiftieth anniversary of its incorporation in 1976, the village could boast of a hospital, a number of doctors, dentists and lawyers, a sprawling school system, a string of motels and restaurants, specialty stores, street lighting, a sewage system, paved streets, and an airplane landing strip a few miles outside the village.

The site which yielded a rich crop of furs sixty years before had moved ahead with the times.

THESE SAME DECADES, the thirties right up to the seventies, brought stagnation to the village of Stoney Creek. There, despite the fact that the number of band members was slowly decreasing, time seemed to have stopped, once and for all, soon after 1920.

Far from holding their heads somewhere above the water line, the people of Stoney Creek, used as they were to depression conditions for all of their lives, found the 1930s to be a desperate time on the reserve. "One time I'll tell you about," said elder Mary John, "both my sister-in-law and I had a batch of kids. Our husbands went trapping and it was in the midst of real hardship.

We were left with nothing. We were just like a dog, you know, you see a dog with puppies, you leave the puppies at home and then you scrounge in the bush, hunting and fishing. That's what we did. From day to day, we made our living that way. I don't know what made us think of the Indian Department—maybe we heard someone talking. We asked the Indian Agent for a ration, so after much argument he gave us a little note. It was a single ration between the two of us and all our children—there was twenty-four pounds of flour, five pounds of sugar, half pound of tea, a bit of salt, a little rice, a little lard. He said not to come back. Oh, well, we were young and really tough. We thought we could tough it out."

Tough it out they did, all the people of Stoney Creek.

Through the next thirty-five or forty years they hunted and fished, cut wood for the stoves of Vanderhoof and ties for the railway. They did roadwork and drove graders for the Department of Highways and they fought fires in the forest fire season. At Pinchi Lake and Endako mines and the Kenney Dam, in the hospital and the motels and restaurants of Vanderhoof they, with few exceptions, held the most menial of jobs and, as often as not, were the first to be laid off when work wound down or when profits dropped.

Through all the years into the 1970s, the settlement along the banks of Stoney Creek was almost untouched by the building, the modernization, that was going on all around.

In time electricity came to the reserve, but in 1976 Stoney Creek settlement had no paved roads or streets, no sewage system, no street lighting, no industry. For a few years there was a school in operation, but after the Department of Indian Affairs hired a series of teachers, many of whom proved to be racist or manic-depressive or just plain bewildered, the school reverted to a kindergarten and the older children were bussed into a school in Vanderhoof or boarded in a Catholic high school in Prince George, seventy miles away. Most of the log shacks had disappeared by 1976, to be replaced by houses which were deceptively modern in appearance—in fact, central heating was non-existent in these homes and only one in five had indoor plumbing.

In 1976 not a loaf of bread, not a quart of milk could be purchased in Stoney Creek—there was no store. Apart from the halcyon years in the fifties when the Kenney Dam was being built, there was no bus service between the village and Vanderhoof.

In 1976 the Natives of Stoney Creek knew that their settlement was an anachronism.

They talked of many things.

They spoke of the tax dollars which poured into the coffers of the Indian Affairs Department year after year, and they talked of how this green flow, like the channel of a river which had been diverted, never seemed to reach them. They looked at the experts in economic development and housing and education whom the federal government hired to plan for the Indians and they wondered how it could be, with so many high-priced professionals busily planning for them, that there was no economic development on Stoney Creek, that their housing program was a travesty and that in all the years up to 1976, only two Carrier in their area had ever graduated from a university.

By 1976 the Natives of Stoney Creek were speaking to each other, and sometimes they even spoke to the country's leaders, about their lack of a sewage system, of the increase of tuberculosis on their reserve, of their desire to take over their own educational system, of their need for a bus service, shopping facilities, a recreation centre for their young people, an industry, perhaps a sawmill, which could replace welfare with employment for the residents of the reserve.

They did not speak of the sun rising in the east each morning, nor of the changing seasons, nor of the leaves dropping from the trees soon after the first frost each autumn, for these things had been a part of their lives since time immemorial.

Nor did they speak in 1976 of the fact that, although Vanderhoof and Stoney Creek were separated by only nine miles, each of these communities was isolated, one from the other, so that the distance might as well have been nine thousand miles. True, the Natives of Stoney Creek spent almost all their money in Vanderhoof, tens of thousands of dollars each month. But this spending of money in white businesses, the attendance of their children in white schools—these things, with few exceptions, did not mean that white people visited the homes in Stoney Creek, or that Natives dropped into white homes in Vanderhoof for a cup of coffee or a beer or a game of cards. It did not mean that when the school day was done, Native children stayed behind to socialize with white students.

The Natives of Stoney Creek, the white citizens of Vanderhoof, did not speak of these things, because this had been the relationship between the two communities for as long as the oldest living person could remember.

In 1976, if the Natives spoke of it at all, they would in all likelihood have said that some things had changed. Vanderhoof restaurants no longer refused them service; no longer did Natives, caught overnight in Vanderhoof, have to find a bed in the hospital because the hotels would not rent a room to them. Yes, Stoney Creek people would say, things like this had changed; they might add that many other places—Burns Lake, Kenora, Kamloops, Prince Albert—were not much better. In all of these places, and many more, they knew that Natives lived as a people apart.

And they would have said, if they thought in these terms, that it was surely not the fault of Vanderhoof that their reserve was poor or that their children seldom got beyond Grade 8 in school. They would have said no, it was not Vanderhoof's fault, but on the other hand, Vanderhoof with its community organizations, its Board of Trade, its church groups, its village council, had never shown much concern either that life had been harsh and degrading and often brutal for the people of Stoney Creek.

These two communities, the one by a wandering busy creek, the other beside the bend in a proud river, each lived in a tight little world of its own. As if carved in marble, the two solitudes seemed doomed to last forever.

AND YET. . . .

In the summer of 1976 beneath an apparently static, even a tranquil surface, there lurked an air of waiting in the land surrounding the Nechako Valley.

And in the early morning hours of July 3, 1976, when tires screeched on a street near the outskirts of Vanderhoof and the body of a young Native girl, within days of giving birth to a child, was lifted by an automobile and then dropped to the pavement, that quiescent surface was shattered.

There was to be little tranquility in Vanderhoof that summer of 1976.

2

THE HOLIDAY WEEKEND OF JULY 1, 1976, promised a gala few days for the Village of Vanderhoof. To commemorate fifty years of incorporation, community leaders joined together to arrange a program which included an old-time dance, a canoe race, a rodeo, a pancake breakfast, a family picnic, an old-timers' reunion tea, and sports events of all kinds. Festivities ended with a street dance which went on until the early hours of the morning of July 3. The nearby settlements of Fort St. James, Fort Fraser, Fraser Lake, and Stoney Creek were nearly empty of people in the rush to join the midsummer celebration. Former residents of Vanderhoof from larger centres nearby, and the lower mainland too, joined with old friends and relatives to eat and talk and reminisce about the good old days when they, and Vanderhoof, were young.

The celebration meant weeks of hard work for many citizens of Vanderhoof; when it was over, these same community leaders could pronounce the celebration a success beyond anything they might have anticipated.

ON JULY 2, COREEN GAY THOMAS, a twenty-one-year-old resident of Stoney Creek and into her ninth month of pregnancy, rented a room in the Vanderhoof Hotel and proceeded to enjoy the street dance with her friends and sisters. Later her friends were to say that after the dance she discovered she had lost the key to her hotel room and was refused another by an employee of the hotel. The manager of the hotel, Sandy Ingram, denied this—Coreen came to him after midnight, he said, and asked if one of her sisters could use the room in her place. Sandy Ingram said that he agreed.

Whatever the reason for Coreen leaving the hotel, sometime after 2:30 in the morning she started out with her sister Margie and a group of friends to walk the nine miles back to the reserve. The early morning air was warm and, despite the fact that Coreen was due to deliver her baby in a matter of days, she and her friends thought nothing of their trek back to the reserve. They had walked the same nine miles hundreds of times before.

Still within the boundaries of Vanderhoof, on a well-lit paved road leading up a hill, Coreen was struck by a car driven by twenty-one-year-old Richard Redekop. Witnesses said that Coreen was carried along by the impact for several feet before being dropped to the pavement. In due course RCMP and an ambulance arrived and, in due course too, Coreen's body was placed in the hospital morgue.

Shortly after four in the morning, a statement was taken from Richard Redekop at the police station and breathalyser tests were administered. He was then allowed to go to the home of his parents, on the road to Stoney Creek.

Two or three hours later, Coreen's fourteen-year-old sister Margie, hysterical and still in a state of shock, was taken back to the reserve by friends. Only when she returned and the church bells began tolling did the people on the reserve learn that death had come to their community again.

When the people of Stoney Creek heard that Coreen had been killed by a car driven by Richard Redekop, they were stunned. Redekop . . . Redekop . . . they spoke the name over and over to themselves. Only two years before, a younger brother of Richard, Stanley Redekop, driving a pickup truck, had struck and killed Coreen's cousin, Larry Thomas. Stoney Creek people had never accepted the verdict of the inquest held after that death. Stoney Creek elders said that the lawyer for the Thomas family was not notified of the hearing until one hour before the jury sat, although he lived sixty miles away in Prince George. Larry Thomas' mother, said the people, was picked up just before the inquest, ostensibly for talking too loudly, lodged in cells and released only when the inquest was over. Most unacceptable of all to the Thomas family and to everyone on the reserve was the jury's decision that no negligence was involved, although the Thomas family believed that there had been too many people in the cab of the truck when Larry Thomas was struck and killed.

The news that another Redekop vehicle had killed another member of the Thomas family went through the reserve like a prairie fire.

Back along the road between Stoney Creek and Vanderhoof where the Redekop family lived, another tragedy was in the making. Seventeen-year-old Bonnie Redekop, sister of Richard and Stanley, was in Prince George hospital, critically injured after being in a car accident a week before. On July 3, just hours after Coreen was killed, young Bonnie Redekop died.

3

SOPHIE THOMAS, CONSIDERED the aunt of Larry and Coreen although the relationship was rather more distant, and president of the Stoney Creek Branch of the Indian Homemakers, was heartsick at the news that Coreen and her baby with her had been killed. As she helped to lay out Coreen and her baby for burial, she was numb with the knowledge that very bad things were happening to her people. All through her life Sophie had worked for better times for the Carrier. Now she wondered: are times better, or are they just as bad for us, just as violent, just as dangerous, as the worst of the bad old days?

Sophie Thomas could look back on many years of Stoney Creek history. Her parents, Pius and Melanie George, died on the reserve in the 1918 flu epidemic when Sophie was only ten months old. She was cared for by her grandmother, Christine John, who was old and nearly blind. "I remember having to lead her around," says Sophie. "I used to walk with her into town which was a nine-mile walk on a wagon trail. It would take about four hours to get to town, but I don't really know as we told time by the sun." Her grandmother taught her the ways of survival. Early on Sophie learned how to place snares and traps for small game and to set nets for fish.

Like so many Native children of her generation, Sophie attended Lejac Residential School from the time she was seven until she was thirteen. Despite the harshness of those years, the hunger, the loneliness, the regimentation that the missionaries and nuns imposed on the homesick fearful children, she says now, "It wasn't so bad." She says that she learned some skills there—among other things she learned to cut out patterns, to make clothes and knit, and to bake bread.

"I remember," says Sophie, "when I used to come home from Lejac, Stoney Creek used to hold a First of July full of events. They would collect donations as prizes from the merchants in Vanderhoof. I won a little suitcase, men's gloves, a pound of tea, in the hundred yard race. My grandmother had to sell the gloves for groceries. We played baseball with homemade bats and bare hands. We had high-jumping events. We had a lot of fun. I was a runner and won in the whole area right up to Smithers. They told me I couldn't beat Mary Jardean. I left her a good fifty yards behind and they started nicknaming me 'the little racehorse.' The people watching couldn't believe how fast I was! I was really a lively person when I was young."

She had two years of freedom before her marriage was arranged, two years in which she followed her relatives to the traplines and hunting grounds. She learned to skin muskrat, fox, and moose. She remembers skinning her first moose: "My uncle gave me a young moose to skin, my first. I kept running back to watch my aunt and uncle skin, and then I would run back to my little moose and do the same. When both sides of the moose were done, I didn't know what else to do. My uncle told me to cut it into quarters. This was the funniest cut I ever made! I still remember where all this took place."

Sophie remembers too the first really big potlatch she attended. She remembers how hard she and her relatives worked to prepare for the potlatch—beaver meat, mallards, fish—all were brought to Sophie's mother's birthplace, Cheslatta, along with pack after pack of tanned moose hides. The potlatch was put on by Sophie's aunt who had lost two sons. A tombstone was being placed on their graves, and a paying out of moose hides and money was made to those who had prepared the two sons' bodies for burial and who sat with the family at the wake which followed the deaths.

When Sophie was fifteen years old, she married twenty-five-year-old Maurice Thomas. Like girls who were her schoolmates—Mary John, Veronica George and the rest—Sophie did not know her husband before she married him. She was equally ignorant about the facts of life. In the Carrier culture it would have been considered unseemly to talk about sex to a young girl of fifteen.

"Yes," says Sophie, "the school wouldn't hold us after we reached fifteen. I wanted to go back to school, but the elders, the Watchmen, they all said I was old enough to get married. Those Watchmen! We don't have them anymore but in those days the old religion, the Catholic religion, was so strong, and the older people didn't want us to run around. They picked these men to watch over all the young people, especially at night. I remember I got fined a dollar by the Watchmen once because I walked out late!"

Although it was no laughing matter at the time, Sophie laughs now about her wedding day. "Imagine! There was no ring, no dress, no nothing. Maurice and I got married and then I went home and I stayed alone for two days. I never went to my husband in those two days; no, I stayed alone. Then a relative of my mother-in-law came and took me home to my husband. He had an old house that had been given to him by his grandfather. The log houses were all in a row and we lived in that one for quite a while."

Sophie's first child, born when she was sixteen years old, died within a few months. Many others were to follow. In all, she gave birth to fifteen children. She talks of the hard times she and Maurice shared in the years after that wedding in 1932. They cleared land (the area where planes now land outside of Vanderhoof was cleared by Sophie and her husband), they cut railway ties, and once many years ago, Sophie remembers how she washed dishes for half a day for Mrs. Murphy, who owned a café. "She gave me a blue suit of clothes," remembers Sophie, "the nicest thing I ever owned. I still remember her kindness."

But many times the family went to bed hungry, says Sophie, and still the babies kept coming. "When we cleared land, I had the children with me. I had to pack them everywhere I worked, even when I chopped a tree, I had one on my back. When I set snares and planted potatoes, I pack two babies and I lead one.

"I remember all the walking I had to do to go to Vanderhoof. Lots of times I cried because I was so tired. I made up my mind. One day I'm not gonna walk this road. It was hard. I made up my mind then to work for my people, so life would be easier. . . . I learned a big lesson, life isn't a bed of roses."

By 1976, Sophie was an acknowledged leader in Stoney Creek village. She was president of the Stoney Creek Homemakers, an association of Indian women formed in the 1940s to improve their skills as housewives and mothers. She was the person who attended conferences around the province and spoke for the Stoney Creek Branch of the Homemakers, and was often a representative for the reserve when communication was necessary with government officials.

Sophie's life, however, was not just made of meetings, conferences, workshops and the like, away from the village. In Stoney Creek when she was at home, which was most of the time, there were her children and grandchildren to help and to guide, and there was a constant coming and going into and out of her home of many young people, nieces and nephews among them. None came more frequently than Coreen, and no one was more welcome.

Coreen was the second eldest of nine children whose father,

Peter, was the cousin of Sophie's husband. Coreen attended St. Joseph's School, riding to school each day in what the white students called "the Indian bus" and which they sometimes pelted with snowballs or whatever weaponry the season of the year might provide for them. Needless to say, these attacks were not forgotten, and street fights could erupt years later when protagonists met on the Vanderhoof streets and past challenges were revived.

Coreen left school when her years at St. Joseph's were done, and from then until that fateful walk in the early morning of July 3, she helped to look after an aging grandmother and her younger brothers and sisters. She was, according to the villagers, a real little mother—no higher compliment could be paid to her. But no matter what chores she had to do, she managed to visit her Aunt Sophie every day. She was surely one of the family.

And Coreen was in love.

She and the boy were really childhood sweethearts. Coreen was of a new generation; she did not have to endure the watchful eyes of elders, as did Sophie and many others with her, nor a dollar fine for staying out late, nor an arranged marriage with a man she did not know. In 1976, when Coreen discovered she was pregnant, rings had been exchanged, and plans for a wedding had already begun.

The white way is not the Native way. "It is against our ways," says Sophie, "to get married [before] the baby is born. They would wait until after the birth, which was our custom."

The wait for the baby's birth, and for the wedding which was to follow, began to seem long as June faded into July in that year of 1976. Coreen's young man was away in Williams Lake, attending the stampede which was an annual event there; all of her friends were back and forth between Vanderhoof and Stoney Creek as the weekend festivities went on. Perhaps her friends coaxed her to come with them. "Come on," they might have said, "it won't hurt you!" Perhaps she thought, "Yes, I'll go to the dance in town. I can rent a room in the hotel and I'll be all right. It will help to pass the time."

And so tragically, almost casually, Coreen went into Vanderhoof towards the end of that holiday weekend.

4

V ERY SOON AFTER MARGIE returned to Stoney Creek to tell her father the news of Coreen's death, Sophie Thomas' phone rang. It was a close friend, Maggie Antoine. She thought that she should be the one to break the bad news to Sophie.

Sophie was incredulous. There must be some mistake . . . not Coreen, she thought brokenly.

Her very first act was to phone the hospital. Sophie's husband Maurice was responsible for ringing the church bell which announced that death had come to the village. She had to be certain of the news before Maurice went off to the church.

"Is Coreen Thomas dead in your hospital?" she asked the hospital employee.

Yes, Sophie was told, really, she is dead.

Sophie's next thought was of Coreen's father, Peter Thomas. My Lord, she thought, what will he do? He will take this very hard; probably the first thing he will do is to go to Vanderhoof to see for himself if Margie's news is right. Within minutes Sophie and one of her sons were driving down the road looking for Peter. Sure enough, there he was on the side of the road heading towards Vanderhoof. And Sophie had foretold his re-action correctly—he was going to the hospital to see for himself. Only then would he believe the news that this beloved child, the apple of his eye, was dead.

Shortly thereafter, the RCMP sent a message out to the reserve: they wanted to interview Margie Thomas and some of the other young people who had been walking with Coreen when she was killed. Sophie and her friend Mary John, Mary's daughter Helen Jones, and Native leader Archie Patrick picked up Margie, Donna Patrick, and some other young witnesses and drove them to the police station in Vanderhoof.

Mary John was known to the young witnesses—she was a comfort to them. Although she was a few years older than Sophie, in many ways their lives had been similar—residential school, an arranged marriage, and the bearing of twelve children, many of them born on the trap line or the hunting grounds. In constrast to Sophie's more public figure, Mary John's efforts had been directed at saving the language and the cultural life of the Carrier people; only the crisis surrounding Coreen's death could force her to move into a more public arena. Mary's daughter Helen, after fifteen years spent in a tuberculosis sanitorium, was now back home in Stoney Creek and was working with Indian students attending school in Vanderhoof. Archie Patrick, one of two Carrier who were university graduates, was also involved in education. He was employed as coordinator of Indian education in the Vanderhoof School District. Helen and Archie went along to the RCMP station because they knew the young people and thought they might help to make the police interrogation less frightening.

Sophie talked to the young people on the way to the station.

"I talked to them in my language," she said afterwards. "I told them that when they make a statement to tell it straight, just what happened and not to use too many words, because they wouldn't be able to remember it all the next time they were questioned."

Mary John remembered that long afternoon.

"I think my bad feelings about the RCMP and the coroner and the way in which they were handling Coreen's death began that afternoon," she says. "The young people were frightened and upset, especially Margie (Marjorie) and Donna. They were taken into a room for questioning. Our request that one of us go in with them was refused. Instead, Sophie, Helen, Archie, and I sat on the steps of the police station for three hours, while the young people were being questioned inside the building. We were not even offered chairs to make our long wait more bearable."

Soon after this uncivil beginning, Sophie read a brief newspaper account of Coreen's death in the *Prince George Citizen*. It troubled her deeply. The report struck her as ominous, for it seemed to foreshadow the way in which that death would be handled by RCMP investigating officers: "A 21-year-old Stoney Creek resident, Coreen Gay Thomas," ran the report, "died when she was hit by a car in Vanderhoof early Saturday. Police said today the woman was walking along Kenney Dam Road near Sixth Street with several other people about 3:35 a.m. when the accident happened. The woman apparently darted in front of a car driven by Richard Brian Redekop, 21, of Vanderhoof, police said. Police are continuing the investigation."

This report contradicted what Margie and Donna Patrick had said to Sophie and Mary John. The girls insisted that Richard Redekop had been driving too fast and that Coreen had no chance to get out of the vehicle's path.

Sophie knew that some action was needed to clear the air, but what? She began to hear rumours that the coroner, Eric Turner, agreed with the RCMP's version of Coreen's death, and that he had decided not to hold an inquest. She knew nothing about Eric Turner except that he had conducted the inquest into Larry Thomas' death two years before—this did little to reassure Sophie—and that he had a real estate business. He seemed to her to be part of the power structure in Vanderhoof that was so remote from the people of Stoney Creek. One of the things she remembered about him was the slogan of his business which she had often read in the local paper: "The Go-Ahead Firm for Look-Ahead People."

In desperation she phoned Rose Charlie, president of the British Columbia Association of Indian Homemakers in Vancouver. "Rose," she said, "I'm in really bad trouble up here. There's been a death and it looks like there isn't going to be an inquest. You better send someone up right away!"

Because of health problems, Rose was not able to make the trip, but within days Kitty Bell, a member of the B.C. Indian Homemakers and active in the publication of *Native Voice*, a newspaper published in Vancouver, was in Stoney Creek. She spent many hours interviewing the young people who had been with Coreen on the night that she was killed. Marjorie Thomas, Donna Patrick, Vincent Sam, Bruce Allan, Barry Quaw—these and many more told the story of that early morning walk to Kitty. From here Kitty Bell conferred with lawyers and with members of the B.C. Human Rights Commission.

The next edition of *Native Voice* opened a veritable Pandora's box in the central interior of British Columbia. It carried two blazing headlines: INDIANS HARASSED ON ROAD and RACISM AND BRUTALITY RAMPANT.

These reports, detailing as they did incidents of harassment on the streets and roads of Vanderhoof, gave the signal for the media, first in Vanderhoof and then around the province, to take up the cause that Sophie Thomas had called her "really bad trouble."

5

THE *NECHAKO CHRONICLE*, published in Vanderhoof, was one of the first newspapers to add fuel to the smouldering situation. On August 12 this newspaper summarized the charges made by Kitty Bell in the July issue of *Native Voice*.

"In two front page stories in the July issue of *Native Voice*," said the *Nechako Chronicle*, "residents of Stoney Creek are quoted as charging harassment by the white population of Vanderhoof. The articles say the village sport after the bars close at night is to barrel down the highway to harass Native people in a game referred to as 'chicken.' . . . The articles state that most people on the Stoney Creek Reserve have experienced this kind of harassment, both young and old members. They also say that complaints to the police last year have resulted in no action. The articles allege that Stanley and Richard Redekop are leaders in the gangs that carry out the harassment. They state that the Native people of Stoney Creek feel that two deaths on the highway have been a direct result of this harassment. . . . A spokesman for the Stoney Creek Band stated to the *Chronicle* that the Natives feel they are not being given adequate police protection. He said that threats to witnesses into the accident have been made with no action being taken by the RCMP."

On the same day Eli Sopow of the *Prince George Citizen* reported that the B.C. Human Rights Branch had turned over the results of a two-week investigation into charges of harassment to the Human Rights Commission. The Commission, wrote Eli Sopow, has given top priority to the investigation, and had the power to involve both the Attorney General's Department and the Police Commission.

Staff Sergeant Hank Dedish of the Vanderhoof RCMP detachment confirmed that the investigation into Coreen's death was continuing. "The file," he said, "is about four inches thick." He added that there was no indication to date that any criminal negligence occurred in the incident.

Within a very few days reports were circulating that the B.C. Human Rights Commission was requesting a meeting with the Police Commission. The Human Rights chairman, Bishop Remi De Roo, told reporters that if even one-half of the reports of Indian abuse by whites in Vanderhoof was true, it was a heartbreaking situation. The Vanderhoof scene, he felt, was explosive, with a potential for "very deep violence."

On August 24, with rumours drifting through Stoney Creek at the speed of light—rumours that both Margie Thomas and Donna Patrick were threatened during their questioning by a police officer, rumours that this same police officer suggested to another witness that his probation might be threatened if he said the wrong things, rumours that despite the fact that Richard Redekop was speeding when his car struck Coreen, the RCMP were determined to make Coreen responsible for her own death on the road—Sophie Thomas met with the Stoney Creek Indian Homemakers. It was decided that she would write to the Vanderhoof coroner, Eric Turner. Sophie complied with this decision. "The Homemakers and band members," she wrote, "are asking for a public inquest. Please advise."

On the day this letter was mailed to Eric Turner, the *Nechako Chronicle* reported in front page headlines that Vanderhoof was the centre of controversy. "An extensive investigation by the RCMP," the *Chronicle* reported, "in which all pertinent witnesses were interviewed was turned over to Coroner Eric Turner. After studying the whole case, Turner decided not to have an inquest as all the facts are at his disposal. On the basis of this information, an inquiry into the death was held and the results of that inquiry have been presented to the Attorney General. Also on the basis of the investigation, no charges have been laid or are contemplated against the driver of the car, Richard Redekop."

The *Chronicle* went on: "The incident is now receiving wide publicity throughout the province and the country. Front page articles are appearing in various newspapers which foretell violence and shooting if the Native call for an inquest is not heard. Kitty Bell, spokesman for the B.C. Indian Homemakers Association, told our paper that the Indian people do not believe there is any justice in Vanderhoof. . . . Bell said that unless justice was done in Vanderhoof, that groups of Natives would be coming to Vanderhoof to see that justice was done. . . . She also said that the very land that Vanderhoof is built on actually belongs to the Indians as part of their Native hunting rights. . . . A spokesman for the Attorney General's Department said this week that the Eric Turner report is being reviewed and a decision will be made in a few days whether to order an inquest in addition to the inquiry."

In fact Eric Turner's report to the Attorney General's Department summarized in a few sentences his judgement on Coreen's death: "The deceased was killed at 3:35 a.m. on July 3, 1976, as a result of being run down by a vehicle driven by Richard Brian Redekop. The deceased, in a drunken condition, darted out in front of the moving vehicle so that collision was inevitable . . . deceased was very drunk, thirty-four weeks pregnant and, according to witnesses, was attempting to play 'chicken' with the vehicle. An analysis of the skid marks showed that the vehicle was travelling at approximately thirty-eight miles an hour and the driver had blood alcohol content of .08 and .05. No charges were laid."

A DAY OR TWO AFTER THE *Chronicle* report, Sophie Thomas and a group of children from Stoney Creek were boarding a bus in Vanderhoof which was to take them to Prince George, where they would perform Native dances at the Catholic high school.

A man stopped near them.

"Is that you, Sophie?" he asked.

"Who are you?" asked Sophie. "I don't know you."

The stranger said that he was the coroner, Eric Turner. "I had never seen him before," said Sophie afterwards.

"Do you really want an inquest?" he asked.

"I told him that is the only way I am going to forget it," Sophie said later. "I can't forget it now. With every death, I told him, they always have an inquest. I don't see why with this, I told him, they don't have one. And then he talked about Bonnie Redekop, Richard's sister, and he said there wasn't an inquest after she died. And I told him that death was accidental, there were too many in the car and they ran into a ramp and that's what killed her. And then again he asked me if I really wanted an inquest. So I told him, that's the only way I'll get it out of my head. I'm really on the warpath! I told him. And he said, 'Sophie, I know you. In that quick second,' he said, 'I made up my mind to give you an inquest.' "

That day Eric Turner explained the events that led up to this decision when he spoke on a local radio station.

"I was notified early in the morning of July 3 that Miss Thomas had been killed on the road leading to the reserve. I attended the scene of the accident and made sure that an adequate investigation was being carried out and kept in close touch as to witnesses called and statements made, scientific evidence such as skid marks, alcoholic content, breathalyser tests. As a result of my inquiry, I felt that I was in full possession of all the facts. I felt straightforward conclusions could be derived from these facts. I felt in my own mind that I knew

47

exactly what happened at the time of her death and as a result, I completed my report of inquiry, which is the normal way. At that time, there was no doubt in my mind as to the cause and nature of the accident.

"I am not prepared and never have been prepared," continued the coroner, "to accept anything that has been dreamed up for positive political motives or for sensational journalism motives and I will never be influenced by these factors."

Touching on his encounter with Sophie Thomas, he said, "I had until today decided that the inquiry I completed was quite adequate and I also stated this to the Attorney General's Department. However today, for the first time since the accident, I received a direct communication from the Indian band through Sophie Thomas. After talking to one or two of the local Indian people, I decided that the local concern did call for an inquest and I advised the Attorney General's Department that I was prepared to call a public inquest."

In fact, the announcement that an inquest would be held was made jointly on September 2 by Eric Turner and the Attorney General's Department. Eric Turner added some details in his announcement. The inquest, he said, would be in the form of a night sitting in order to accommodate a number of witnesses. He went on: "My decision to call for an inquest was in no way based on the incendiary sensational journalism that the press has been guilty of. I will never be swayed by people irresponsible in journalism or people politically or violently motiviated."

At the same time, in answer to questions from reporters, a spokesman from the Attorney General's Department said that certainly there would be Natives on a six-member jury.

On this same day, September 2, the Human Rights Commission met with the Police Commission in Victoria. After the meeting Human Rights chairman Bishop De Roo confirmed that the joint meeting had identified many problems existing in the province. He recognized, he said, that the Vanderhoof situation was part of a much deeper social problem. "We must ask ourselves," said the chairman, "why there are two systems of justice—why many Native Indians find themselves in jail on the same charges that many whites are released on."

The problems, he added, were not new.

The next day, September 3, newspapers across the province carried another headline—the Indian Homemakers had asked Harry Rankin, noted lawyer and Vancouver alderman, to represent their organization at the inquest. Harry Rankin had agreed. This colourful and controversial figure added another dimension to the Coreen Thomas story. From the time Rankin was called to the bar, he had made headlines. Most recently, he had acted for the Natives in what became known as the Fred Quilt affair, an inquest into the death of a Chilcotin Indian who died while in police custody. At that time, Rankin was called before the Law Society to answer for statements he had made to the Indian Band to the effect that the police didn't mind beating up an Indian, but that they didn't like to get caught. On the day in which the Law Society met in Vancouver to decide his fate, a demonstration of hundreds of Rankin supporters, fearing that he would be disbarred, had circled the building in which the Law Society met. The charge was dismissed. Now the news that this man was to represent the B.C. Indian Homemakers at the upcoming inquest sent ripples of excitement, and, it must be added, a few shudders through the community of Vanderhoof.

Eli Sopow reported in the *Prince George Citizen*: "Rankin said in a telephone interview today that no one should set any specific time limits on the inquest. . . . 'An inquest,' said Rankin, 'should last as long as necessary to find out when, where and how as people were to sensation upon sensation that summer, no one was prepared for the headlines in newspapers across the province on September 8. Seemingly almost by accident, a former

newspaper reporter from Prince George put two and two together about events of ten years before and suddenly Eric
Turner, rather than Coreen Thomas, was the one making the
headlines. VANDERHOOF CORONER RECALLS OWN CON-
VICTION TEN YEARS AGO; VANDERHOOF CORONER WITH-
DRAWS FROM INQUEST; TURNER WANTS OUT—these were
a few of the leaders in papers across the province that day. When
these headlines appeared, Bob Harkins, a Prince George radio
personality and alderman, was fit to be tied—he had gone to his
news editor at the time Turner was refusing an inquest into
Coreen's death and said, "There's a story here! This guy Turner
was in a hit-and-run himself a few years ago!" His editor
evidently didn't think the story sufficiently newsworthy and so
the scoop came later and from another reporter.

Berton Woodward wrote in the *Vancouver Province*: "The
Vanderhoof coroner . . . was convicted of a criminal charge arising from a hit-and-run death about ten years ago. Coroner Eric
Turner confirmed that he drove away after hitting and killing a
man on a highway near Prince George and didn't report the
accident until the next morning. Associate Deputy Attorney
General Alex Pearson, calling the situation 'most unusual,' said
the department would investigate and would check why an RCMP
report on Turner made just before his appointment in May,
1972, did not include the information."

The *Vancouver Province* report continued: "Turner confirmed
that he was convicted but said that he could not remember the
exact charge. He thought it was public mischief and that he was
fined $300. He also said that he could not remember exactly
when the accident occurred nor the victim's name, but believed
that it happened about ten years ago. Describing the incident,
Turner said he was driving late on a stormy night when a
drunken white man staggered in front of the car. . . 'I woke up
in a cold sweat for three years after, seeing that body shoot over

my windshield,' said Turner. He said he panicked and drove home, then turned himself in in the morning. 'I never believed that things like that really happened—people panicking, going into a state of shock. It really does happen. You just quit thinking and go on blind instinct.' Turner said the accident is known in the community. 'I worked ever since then to atone for it by being a good citizen and helping out far more than the ordinary citizen would do.' "

Asked by the reporter if the RCMP knew of this incident, Turner said that he told Sgt. L.A. 'Stretch' McLean, then head of the Vanderhoof detachment, the details during an interview before his appointment as coroner in 1972.

The *Province* article went on: "McLean, now a staff sergeant with the Prince George force, said Tuesday he was aware of the accident but did not know of the charges in the case."

The next day, September 9, Eric Turner was again the subject of front page news articles. In those articles he denied that the story of his accident had been a major factor in his decision to step down as coroner of the impending inquest, but he added that he had been put under some strain by the media dredging up incidents eleven years old.

"Why the hell I or any other coroner would want the job, I just don't know," he said. "The whole purpose of this inquest is being lost because of all the publicity. This is turning into a circus! I'm just wondering if I should have ordered a big tent and some elephants!"

The editor of the *Nechako Chronicle* in Vanderhoof, who also doubled as the local ambulance driver, entered the controversy. He wrote an editorial praising Eric Turner:

"The recent and continuing load of criticism being directed against Eric Turner is perhaps the nastiest bit of work which has been seen locally for quite a while. Turner made a mistake some years ago. At no time did he try to cover that mistake up or say that he did not in fact hit and kill a white person near Prince

George in 1965. His mistake at the time was that he panicked and took off from the scene of the accident. At that time, Turner was tried and convicted of leaving the scene of an accident. He paid the fine imposed and has lived the life of a model citizen since. The accident itself was just that, an accident. According to the records, the person who was killed was jumping in front of cars trying to get them to stop. Turner just happened to be unlucky enough to hit him."

The editorial continued: "All of this happened over ten years ago, yet now the Indian movement is dredging up the old history in an effort to disfame [sic] Eric Turner in his public and thankless job as coroner. . . . Turner has been a fair and impartial coroner at all times. His record, according to the Attorney General, has been a good one and he has had more than his share of cases to handle. We do not think it is fair that a person trying to do a good job in a very demanding public service be subject to innuendo and abuse such as Turner has received. Such action by the Indian movement indicates their lack of respect for other people in their efforts to get their own way. It is our considered opinion that Eric Turner paid for his mistake some years ago and that his transgression should not be held against him. 'Judge not, lest thyself be judged.' "

One Native, whose voice was lost in the sound and fury, said, "I don't know why they call the guy Eric Turner killed a white man. I knew him, his name was Shelley, maybe Peter Shelley, and he was no white man—he was Métis or Cree or something, from Alberta I think. I wonder, why do they keep calling him a white man?"

When the press asked Harry Rankin for a comment, he said that he thought specific details of the highway death in which Eric Turner was involved should be made public. "A question that should be asked," he said, "is why the RCMP did not investigate Turner's criminal record in his application for coroner."

Meanwhile the Attorney General's Department affirmed that an investigation into the matter of Turner's appointment would be made.

Meanwhile too, Eric Turner pondered his future as a coroner. He told the press that the Thomas death was seriously affecting his business and his home life. "It has been an emotional drain," he said. "It is unfair to put my family through this strain. Office work is falling behind and my house chores are behind—I don't know yet if I will continue as a full-time coroner. It is something I will have to think about and consult with the Attorney General's Department about."

AS ERIC TURNER RUMINATED on the subject of his future relationship with the Attorney General's Department, the department announced that the inquest into Coreen Thomas' death would be held on September 25 at Vanderhoof Secondary School. Presiding would be Glen McDonald, Supervisor of Coroners for British Columbia.

"Like everyone else in Stoney Creek," said Mary John, "I breathed a sigh of relief when I heard about the change of coroners. I hoped that with Mr. McDonald presiding, Native concerns would get a full hearing."

Sophie Thomas was relieved at the news too. But she was still on the warpath. "I'm getting madder every day!" she told a *Globe and Mail* reporter. "If Coreen was not a Native girl this all would have been treated differently!"

Judith Timson of *Maclean's Magazine* visited Vanderhoof that summer and in an article entitled "Two (Bitter) Solitudes" wrote: "Coreen was nine months pregnant when she died. During the autopsy they removed the baby and Coreen's relatives buried her with her unborn baby in her arms. 'That really hurt the Indian people,' recalls Sophie Thomas. 'They really shed a tear when they saw that baby.' But what hurt the Indian people more was their deepening conviction that Coreen's death was another sad chapter in a continuing story of harassment between whites and Indians in a town characterized by several members of both races as being 'one of the most prejudiced towns in the province.' "

Judith Timson's article went on to point out that Richard Redekop was already caught up in the wheels of the justice system—he was facing a court date on December 16, charged with assaulting a Native woman with an aluminum crutch.

The reporter talked to Richard's mother, Linda Redekop.

"How could they think that our boy, after standing over his dying sister, could have thought of killing someone else?" said Mrs. Redekop. "If it hadn't been for our daughter Bonnie's funeral, we would have gone to visit the Thomases and I guess we still should have. I understand how terrible they must be feeling. Why did it have to be one of ours again, and why did it have to be one of theirs? I'll freely admit my sons are scrappers," she went on, "they walk around with their fists up. But we are appalled at the accusations the Indian community has levelled at our family."

AND STILL THE STORIES WENT ON.

The most worrisome, because neither whites nor Natives knew quite what to believe, was a report which alleged that Coreen's mother, Matilda Thomas, had been severely beaten on September 2 in an effort to keep her away from the inquest. This report said that she had been terrified of relating the incident to the RCMP but that she had eventually talked to a white man who was married to a Stoney Creek band member.

She also talked to Sophie Thomas, who said that "two white men came over from a pickup truck and one beat her while the other watched. She had to go to the hospital and still has bad chest pains. Matilda is afraid to go to the police."

Reporters, checking hospital records, confirmed that Matilda Thomas was treated in the emergency ward of the hospital in Vanderhoof on September 2.

Harry Rankin was incensed when he heard of this latest incident. My inclination now," he said, "is to ask the Attorney General's Department to send up a special investigator to Vanderhoof to find out what's going on."

The supervisor of Coroners, Glen McDonald, who was slated to preside at the inquest, was reported to have said that he would ask to have Coreen's mother placed in protective custody. By September 13 McDonald denied having contemplated making any such request. At the same time a spokesman for the RCMP said that Mrs. Thomas had been questioned and it had been established that, although she received a kick from an unknown assailant who then fled the scene, no threats pertaining to the inquest had been made.

Harry Rankin expressed skepticism when he heard the RCMP version of what came to be called the 'Matilda Thomas story.' "I believe the charges attributed to Mrs. Thomas," he said. "Indians are not going to the police because they do not trust them."

ELDER MARY JOHN SAID LATER, "It seemed to me that we never stopped in those weeks between July 3 and September 25. For the first time, people like Sophie Thomas and my daughter Helen and Archie Patrick, a Native teacher, had a chance to tell the world what living conditions were really like in our village."

Sophie Thomas spoke about the band members' fears that disease was on the increase. "We have at least ten cases of tuberculosis," she said, "and that's on the reserve with a population of four hundred Indians. I read that that's about twenty times as high as the rate in the places where white people live."

She went on to talk about the terrible housing conditions on

Stoney Creek Reserve. It was not unusual, she said, for twelve to sixteen people to live in a small two-bedroom house with no proper sanitation. She described one old woman who was sick and who had to crawl on all fours in the winter to the outside toilet because there were no facilities for her inside the house.

"There is very poor sanitation in places, no sewers and a great fear the disease will spread," said Sophie.

Reporters contacted the federal agencies responsible for medical care and housing for Native people. Yes, confirmed Dr. G.C. Butler, Regional Director for the Federal Medical Services Division, there had been six new cases and four relapsed cases of tuberculosis on the Stoney Creek Reserve in the first five months of the current year. He added that the cases seemed to be under control and that most victims were being treated in their homes. In answer to another question, he described tuberculosis as "an infectious disease with a greater possibility of spreading in overcrowded living conditions."

When Sophie talked about the federal government's housing policy, her voice became bitter. "We get a subsidy of ten thousand dollars to build a house and it is almost impossible for band members to finance the rest. We need more than ten thousand dollars to construct a house. Prices are going up all the time and it is hard for Indians to find work. I know that Stoney Creek is one of the poorest reserves and it is because there is little employment nearby for the men."

A spokesman for the Department of Indian Affairs made a statement about departmental policy on housing for reserves. "We are aware," he said, "that a lot of agonizing has occurred over the amount of the subsidy but it is a Canada-wide policy and Parliament decided the extent of funds allocated for housing."

Parliament had spoken and that seemed to be that.

7

"SEPTEMBER 25, 1976," said Mary John later, "was one of those fall days in central British Columbia that I loved even as a little girl—the sun had burned off the early morning fog by the time we arrived at the gymnasium of the secondary school in Vanderhoof, and we knew that the day was going to be as warm as a day in July."

She and her daughter Helen watched as people settled into the hard seats the school building provided. Close to them was Sister Paul, an elderly Irish nun who was a teacher in the kindergarten in Stoney Creek Village.

Thirty-two witnesses were to be called, twenty residents from Stoney Creek, twelve from the nearby farms and houses of the town. The media seemed to be everywhere—newspaper and magazine reporters from across the province and the whole of Canada as well, TV personnel, a young man from the local radio station, photographers, representatives from Native newspapers. People performing a watchdog role moved into the gymnasium: staff from the Legal Services Commission from Vancouver, politicians and former politicians, representatives of Native Courtworkers and the United Native Nations, Bishop Remi De Roo and other representatives from the Human Rights Commission, the Department of Indian Affairs.

The lawyers were there—cool, competent Cliff Macarthur appointed by the Attorney General to lead the evidence; mild, lean Murray Miller appearing for Coreen's family; Sid Simons, jaunty in leather jacket and cowboy boots, appearing for Richard Redekop, his wife never more than a whisper away from him; Harry Rankin, his personal trademark, as one reporter commented, of a strong nose and a walrus moustache much in evidence, his law student son-in-law at his side.

Coreen's family was there, her mother and silver-haired father and Sophie Thomas, her strong features marked by years of poverty and hard work.

And Richard Redekop was there with his family, pale and still, his shoulder-length hair neat, his face a study in non-expression.

There was a stir. Glen MacDonald, the Supervisor of Coroners, entered, heavy-set, benign, and ruddy. He was followed by the jury members, six of them, two whites and four Natives. The jury foreman, Chief Ken Luggi from a neighbouring band a few miles to the west of Vanderhoof and normally employed as a Native counsellor for Canada Manpower, took his seat. His five jurors followed suit.

The gymnasium itself, a replica of ten thousand high school gymnasiums across Canada, was acoustically more suited to basketball games and cheerleaders than to an inquest. Echoes reverberated against walls; the whispers of people, even their breathing, produced a steady and persistent hum that formed a backdrop to every word and every speech. All through the day and the evening which followed, people drifted in and out, many of the Natives seeming to prefer the bleachers at the back, the whites keeping closer to the action near the coroner and the lawyers. To one side, eighteen or twenty people crowded around the press table, shuffling pencils and pads and grumbling about the ban on smoking.

Outside the gymnasium floor, the ladies of Vanderhoof did a thriving business—Vanderhoof lacked a concert piano and it was hoped that the sale of coffee and soft drinks, sandwiches, and doughnuts would beef up the piano fund. For four days this sale went on; the best customers, said one of the women, were the RCMP who paced the hallways with dogged attention, and the children who drifted in and out through the wide doors. Never far away from the surging crowd in the hallway was Eric Turner, undersized and perennially tanned, talking now to a police officer, now to a Native elder, as people milled around the gymnasium entrance and the snack table.

THE INQUEST OPENED AT 9:10 A.M. with the traditional call from the sheriff: "You good men and women of this country summoned to appear this day to enquire for our Sovereign the Queen how, where and by what means Coreen Gay Thomas came to her death, answer to your names as you shall be called, every man at the first call, upon the pain and peril that shall fall thereon."

Certain preliminaries followed.

Jury members identified themselves, lawyers made themselves known, and Sid Simons made a rather perfunctory objection to Harry Rankin's presence at the inquest, an objection the coroner instantly denied. A letter from Attorney General Garde Gardom establishing the legal basis for the inquest was read aloud.

Constable Neil Allan Taylor of the RCMP, a thin-faced man appearing to be in his early thirties, with a small moustache and a receding hairline, took the stand. Cliff Macarthur rose to question him.

The inquest had begun.

8

QUESTIONS FROM CLIFF MACARTHUR established that Constable Taylor had been a police officer for seven years and seven months and that he had been stationed in Vanderhoof for just three months.

"Jesus!" whispered one reporter to another, counting back on his fingers. "He must have been here just a week or two when Coreen was killed. What a hell of a mess to walk into!"

"What," asked Cliff Macarthur, "did you do in connection with the matter before this inquest?"

"At approximately 3:30 a.m. on the 3rd of July, 1976," said Constable Taylor, "I responded to a call of a motor vehicle accident. En route to the accident scene I stopped at the Chevron station in Vanderhoof where I picked up a Mr. Redekop . . . who flagged us down and advised that he had called the police and he had been driving a vehicle that ran into a pedestrian."

"And did you make some observations as to his condition at that time?"

"I noted Mr. Redekop to be concerned and attentive concerning the accident," replied the constable. "I noted him to be very alert and he seemed to be stable and steady. I never observed him to walk, so I can't give a description of that . . . I thought he was quite sober. I could smell a very faint odour of alcohol on his breath, but not substantial to indicate he had been drinking extensively."

Constable Taylor added that Mr. Redekop was with his wife,

Faye Haugen, and a small child. Faye Haugen, he said, appeared to be sober.

The constable went on to describe the accident scene.

"As I approached the location I observed several people standing on different parts of the road. At the time it was dark. The pavement was dry. It was partly overcast. I observed street lamps on the east side of Kenney Dam Road, one prior to the intersection of 6th Street and one further south approximately one hundred yards."

"What was the speed limit on that road?"

"Thirty miles an hour."

"Is it posted?"

"No, it is not. On my arrival," continued the constable, "I immediately stopped the car and proceeded to a group of people that was standing and kneeling in the middle of the road, where I approached a person that was lying prone on the road. Her feet were to the north and her head to the south, lying uphill. This person was identified to me by Margie Thomas as being her sister Coreen Thomas. I immediately attempted to see if this person was breathing or not. I felt or checked for pulse on her wrist, carotid artery, and on her temple without success. In my opinion she was deceased at that time. . . . "

Constable Taylor was asked to describe the individuals at the scene and to comment, as much as he was able, on their sobriety.

"The first would have been Margie Thomas," he answered. "She is approximately fourteen-fifteen years of age. She is a Native girl. She was—I noted her to be quite hysterical on my arrival. She was crying and her state of sobriety—I did not think she had been drinking."

One by one the constable named the witnesses. Among the Natives, he said, was Donna Patrick, fifteen years old, who did not appear to have been drinking; Lawrence Johnny, drunk;

Cecil Raphael, twenty-eight or thirty years of age, drunk; Allen Sam, fifteen or sixteen, quite sober; George Barton Patrick, approximately eighteen years of age, drunk; Charlie Johnny, in a drunken condition; Bruce Allan, seemingly sober.

He turned to his recollection of the white witnesses and Natives who appeared to be part of the white group in that early morning of July 3. There was Henry Reddecopp, said the constable, no relation to Richard Redekop, and in an intoxicated state. With Henry Reddecopp was Mark Cormack, under the influence of alcohol but not drunk enough to warrant arrest; Nicholas Friemark, eighteen years of age, under the influence of alcohol but not drunk; Michelle Stewart, a Native girl living in Vanderhoof, fifteen years of age, apparently sober; Kevin (Shorty) Inkster, under the influence of alcohol but not drunk.

"As I was taking the names of witnesses," continued Taylor, "the ambulance arrived and just as this was occurring I observed Constable Reed to mark on the pavement where the body was lying—marking both her head and her feet—where they were. After the ambulance had removed the body of Coreen Thomas from the scene I remained with Constable Harold Bowes to take measurements and take photographs of the accident scene."

Copies of photographs were distributed to jury members and lawyers. Constable Taylor identified them as being photographs taken of the road, the skid marks, the Redekop vehicle, on the morning of July 3.

Helen Jones, sitting close to her mother, shuddered. She had seen the photographs.

The constable outlined the details which must accompany an investigation into any motor vehicle accident that results in a death. He arranged for Constable Reed to take Richard Redekop, along with Miss Haugen and their child, to the police station to arrange a breathalyser test. While this was going on, Constable Taylor took more pictures and measurements at the scene of the accident, had Coreen's mother pointed out to him as she walked up the hill with a friend and advised her of her daughter's death, arranged for the Redekop vehicle to be towed to a centre for safekeeping and inspection and then, finally, he returned to the police station where he interviewed Richard Redekop. Repeated the constable, "On interviewing Mr. Redekop, I noted him to be alert, quite attentive and quite concerned about the accident."

"YOUR HONOUR," SAID CLIFF Macarthur, "we have reached that point in the evidence where we could proceed to take a view of the scene as I believe Your Honour wishes. I would propose we do that and then my friends could possibly cross-examine the witness after we are through."

The coroner had something else on his mind—one of the doors had an obstreperous hinge.

"Counsel, I have just sent my deputy to put some oil on that door," he said. "I think we will get along a lot better when that is done . . . we are going to break for coffee anyhow."

Harry Rankin wanted to clarify matters. "I take it it is just a view [of the accident scene] and the officer pointing out anything that is relevant."

"Yes," said the coroner. "I won't be there myself, I have seen the place. It is just a trip and I hope that the fog is cleared so that you can in fact see Nechako and 6th Avenue."

Harry Rankin wasn't quite satisfied. "Maybe you should be there because sometimes there is some discussion."

The coroner was adamant. "If I am there I am going to have to bring the Court Reporter and everyone. I just think it is a viewing. The more ignorant I stay the more intelligent I get sometimes," he said with a smile. "We will adjourn until eleven o'clock."

As the jurors and lawyers filed into a waiting bus and as others settled into cars which would take them to the accident scene, Barbara Kobierski, originally from the Capilano Reserve and now representing the Legal Services Commission, huddled in one of the moving cars and scribbled in her notebook, "Constable Taylor old core policeman—would draw a hard line—stood giving evidence, legs astride, hands on belt, loud voice. Referred to Natives as drunk, whites as intoxicated."

When everyone was assembled midway up Kenney Dam Hill, Constable Taylor explained the scene of the accident, pointing to lampposts, the spot where he had found Coreen's body, the long stretch of road where skid marks had been found, and the nearest house, a log structure partly hidden by trees. The media's cameras captured the scene which would be flashed across television sets across the country later that evening: Constable Taylor, his arms outstretched, his uniform correct in every detail; Harry Rankin, hands in pockets, looking off into the distance; the jurors, their faces intent, watching Taylor's every gesture. Native juror Sally Erickson trembled as she watched the constable and listened to his description of the sights and sounds of that fatal night. Suddenly, it had all become agonizingly real to her. She couldn't wait to get away from that spot and back into the gymnasium.

WHEN THE INQUEST RECONVENED the coroner elaborated on the duty of the jurors: discovery, to the best of their abilities, of the when, where, how, and after what manner the deceased came to her death. "Putting it another way," said the coroner, "if Coreen Thomas was here, would she ask this question, 'How come I am dead?' "

Constable Taylor was still on the stand. The coroner called on Sid Simons or Harry Rankin to commence the cross-examination.

Said Sid Simons, "I will certainly defer to the seniority of my friend."

Answered Harry Rankin, "You don't have to if you don't want to!"

"I don't have to," retorted Simons, "but I learned it from him!"

The reporters looked knowingly at one another. The slight exchange served to remind insiders that Sid Simons had articled under Harry Rankin and, in fact, had been connected with Rankin's firm in Vancouver for a number of years until the two came to a parting of the ways. This early in the inquest it was apparent that there was going to be no forensic small talk, no social chit-chat between these two contenders.

Harry Rankin leaned into the table before him, his moustache bristling towards the constable in the witness stand. From his first question, it was clear that the lawyer wanted to establish who, in the bureaucracy of the RCMP, evaluated evidence with a view to laying charges.

In answer to the first questions, Constable Taylor responded that four constables, including himself, were involved in the initial accident investigation. Constable Reed was at the scene of the accident, observed details there, took names of witnesses, took Richard Redekop to the police station, and forwarded a sample of Coreen Thomas' blood to the city analyst. Constable Davis performed the breathalyser test on Richard Redekop. Constable Bowes, together with Taylor, took measurements and photographs at the scene of the accident.

"Would you classify that as a thorough investigation from the point of view of your duties as an officer?" asked the lawyer.

"Yes, I would."

Rankin established that Constable Taylor prepared two reports and forwarded them, one in July and one in August, to his superiors in Victoria and Prince George, where they were studied by readers.

The questioning backtracked to the morning of the accident.

"Twenty-nine to four [on the morning of July 3] that you picked up Richard Redekop and headed out to the scene?"

"Yes."

"And that would take a minute or two to get there?"

"Yes."

"As soon as you put your hand on her [Coreen's] pulse you knew she was dead. Why was it there was an hour or more before the person—that is, the driver of the car—was sent down for a breathalyser?"

The constable disagreed with this timetable. "I don't think it was an hour before this person who drove the car arrived at the office for a breathalyser. As I said, I picked up Mr. Redekop at the service station, attended the accident scene—at that time I determined Miss Thomas was deceased. She was taken from the scene and at that time I instructed Constable Reed to take Mr. Redekop to the police station for a breathalyser which he did. I remained at the scene with Constable Bowes and took measurements of the accident scene."

"But you were the officer in charge," insisted Rankin. "You were the man that supplied the interim report and you were the man who would be supplying the final report?"

"Yes."

"Surely an hour—a full hour elapsed before the breathalyser test was given . . . surely it was quite a bit later . . . ?"

Sid Simons was becoming impatient. "Can't we get this through the breathalyser technician?"

Harry Rankin turned on him. "Yes, we can," he said sharply, "but I will get it from this witness!"

Patiently, Constable Taylor outlined the facts of life for an RCMP detachment operating in a small town. "The breathalyser technician was Constable Davis who was not working," he explained. "He was at home and I had to call him at his residence and have him drive to the police office and set up the instrument

66

and perform the test. Mr. Redekop was taken down to the police station at approximately ten minutes to four, I believe, or thereabouts. I wasn't in attendance when Constable Davis arrived so I cannot give an evaluation of that."

"Do you know what the breathalyser reading [for Redekop] was?" queried Rankin.

"Yes. The first reading was .08 and the second reading taken twenty minutes later was .05 per cent."

Continued questioning by Harry Rankin brought an agreement from the police officer that, since the human body normally oxidizes alcohol at the rate of .015 per hour, Richard Redekop's breathalyser reading could have been .095 at the time of the accident.

Having arrived at this point, Harry Rankin burrowed in. "Is that in your report to Prince George and Victoria?" he asked.

"In what report?"

"That having looked at the reading whenever it was taken, the reading was .08 and that having regard to the circumstances when you first saw Richard Redekop, it would be another .015 approximately on top of that?"

"I never put that in my report. I think that any senior officers and their readers are quite well-versed in the points of law and would be able to determine from the time the accident occurred that Mr. Redekop's breathalyser reading would be a certain degree higher. I didn't state in the report that Mr. Redekop would have blown a .095 or a .10 an hour previously."

Harry Rankin stopped, looked at his watch, shuffled his papers.

"I hope he gets off that breathalyser kick," muttered a young radio announcer at the press table. "I never know what the hell they are talking about when they get into oxidation and percentages and all the rest of that crap!"

HARRY RANKIN PICKED UP the Motor Vehicle Accident Investigation Report signed by Constable Taylor. Quoting from the report he read, " 'Vehicle travelling excessive speed when hit.' Whose words are those?"

"They are mine."

"How did you get those words?"

"On to paper . . . I just. . . . "

"From whom did you get those words?" asked the lawyer impatiently. "I know you got them on to paper! You wrote them!"

"From observing or talking to witnesses at the time and getting their summation of the accident scene. That is, I correlated from where Coreen had been standing, where the vehicle came from, and the way I interpreted the accident scene."

Back went Rankin to his central question: "Is it your duty as an investigating officer," he asked, "to recommend whether or not charges will be laid?"

"I may suggest charges."

"In this case, did you recommend charges?"

"I did not recommend charges," said Constable Taylor.

THE LAWYER TURNED to the speed of the Redekop vehicle. Together he and the constable canvassed the opinion of witnesses as outlined in various statements—Henry Reddecopp's statement said the vehicle was travelling at forty-five to fifty miles per hour at the time of impact; Mark Cormack estimated the speed at fifty to sixty miles per hour; Lawrence Johnny, fifty miles per hour; Margie Thomas, seventy miles per hour.

Were these estimates of speed summarized, asked the lawyer, for the readers in the RCMP office in Prince George?

"They can gather that information from the statements," said the constable. "That is not summarized in a paragraph of its own."

Rankin shrugged his shoulders, as if to say, "Let's try something else." He turned to the subject of skid marks.

One way to test speed, he suggested, was to measure the skid marks and arrive at an opinion about speed. Another way would be to take a car out on the same road or hill, run it at various speeds, put on the brakes at a particular spot and see where it stops. Constable Taylor agreed that was another recognized way, after the event, to test for speed.

"Why didn't you run a car up the road, because speed was one of the big issues here, wasn't it?" asked Rankin.

"From the skid marks that were present at the scene of the accident," replied Taylor, "and the measurement of those skid marks I did not feel after consulting with Constable Bowes, who is qualified in this field—I did not feel it necessary to take skid mark tests."

"Why did you believe the lower speed—or did you believe the higher speed given to you in all those statements?"

They argued, the constable and the lawyer, about the meaning of the skid marks, and their confirmation or otherwise of statements made by witnesses that the Redekop vehicle had been going fifty, sixty, as much as seventy miles an hour when Coreen was struck.

And finally, the lawyer came back to his original question—did Constable Taylor make a recommendation that charges be laid?

"No."

"You recommended against it?"

"I wouldn't say 'recommend,' I said that I wouldn't lay charges under these circumstances for a number of reasons."

The lawyer raised finger after finger. "Excessive speed, liquor at least .1, a death on the road. . . . "

"Yes."

"Tell me," said Rankin, "what *does* a person who is driving in the village of Vanderhoof have to do to get charged?"

JUST BEFORE THE LUNCH BREAK, Rankin turned to Taylor's interrogation of Redekop immediately after Coreen's death. He suggested to the constable that he had been very gentle. Taylor disagreed. "I may have used a loud voice on several different questions as to how much he had to drink . . . who he was . . . how long he had lived in Vanderhoof. . . . "

"You knew by your observation that he was going a good deal more than thirty?"

"Ten miles an hour is not a good deal—it is going faster than thirty, yes."

"Forty to forty-five miles is fifteen miles above the speed limit. You knew there had been a death and you knew that he had been drinking?"

"Yes."

"I would suggest," said Rankin, "that if you were serious about your investigation that you would bear down on that point as you have done with a couple of Indian witnesses." He sat down.

Sid Simons jumped to his feet. "Your Honour, I would have to object!"

The coroner interjected, ignoring the moment of acrimony between the two lawyers. "I think we have done a fair morning's work." He turned to Sid Simons. "How long do you think your examination will take?"

"Not nearly as long as my learned friend," said Simons jauntily.

"Adjourned until 1:30," said the coroner.

9

THE SUN WAS BRILLIANT, very nearly blinding, when lawyers and RCMP officers, reporters and spectators, streamed out of the gymnasium at the lunch hour. On this first day of the inquest, the RCMP and many of the lawyers, with a few reporters tagging along, seemed to prefer the polished interior of the Marab Dining Room. The young crowd flocked to the counters of the Tastee Freez. The more mature Natives avoided both the Marab and the Tastee Freez; they preferred the familiarity of the Vanderhoof Hotel. Here, with a sprinkling of whites which included Harry Rankin and his son-in-law, they rehashed the evidence of the morning. The kitchen of the hotel turned out the special of the day—hamburger deluxe platters—more quickly than the proprietor Ruth Ingram would have thought possible.

It was, in fact, the busiest noon-hour trade the restaurants of Vanderhoof had enjoyed since the fiftieth anniversary celebration nearly three months before.

Long before the inquest was reconvened after the lunch break, reporters had scattered in all directions searching for local colour. At the door of the gymnasium a CBC reporter found a Vanderhoof woman willing to be quoted.

"What do you think of the proceedings so far?" asked the reporter.

The white woman shrugged off the question. She was more concerned with the false picture of Vanderhoof which had been painted by the media. Not everyone, she said, should be con-

71

demned for the actions of a few, and she certainly did not agree with the media's statements that Vanderhoof was one of the most racially troubled towns in Canada.

"I have lived here for twenty-five years," she said firmly, "and I have found a wonderful relationship, especially between the old-timers, the people who have lived here for a long time. Personally, I have many friends among the Native people and this is not unusual. It is a natural thing. I think that a lot of people coming in are deliberately putting racial connotations on what is going on in Vanderhoof, but believe me, it isn't a thing that is any worse here than anywhere else. It is no good wherever it is, but it is no worse here."

AT 1:35 SID SIMONS began his examination of Constable Taylor.

Almost immediately he asked, "Sir, if the circumstances here in your investigation were such that they were identical in all respects to your investigation and your findings, save that the deceased lady lying on the road was a white person and the driver of the car was a Native person, would your judgement as to your enquiry and your recommendation be any different than it was?"

"No," said Taylor.

"Is there any question in your mind of that, sir?"

"No."

Simons questioned the constable about the first communication he received that there had been an accident. Taylor confirmed, in answer to questions, that he had followed standard practices in everything he did once he knew that a death was involved.

"In other words," queried Simons, "you didn't treat him [Redekop] any differently than you would have treated anyone else?"

"No."

The constable pointed out that policing the town of Vanderhoof on the night of the accident, with the fiftieth birthday celebration in full swing, had required a good many judgement calls. "I would say," he said, "that the people got a little drunker than they usually do. There was no way that we as a police force in a detachment of this size could have incarcerated all the persons who were intoxicated to such an extent that they should have been incarcerated."

Simons wanted to enlarge on this. "If they seemed able to care for themselves and looked after themselves or if there was someone to look after them, you allowed them to go their own way?"

"That is correct."

"Would you say that applied equally to citizens of Native origin and citizens of Caucasian origin?"

"Yes."

Questioning continued.

"Would you agree that you have had a lot of reports given to you by persons that in your opinion were designed to stir up animosity between the Native and the white population in the Vanderhoof area?"

"Yes."

"For example, it was reported to you by someone that the reason Richard Redekop struck that girl on the road was that he was the father of her child?"

Reporters at the press table suddenly became more attentive. The Thomas family and Mary John shifted angrily in their seats. They knew what was coming. The rumours about Richard Redekop's supposed paternity of Coreen's expected baby had reached Stoney Creek weeks ago. The people from the reserve could name the father of Coreen's child; so, they knew, could Constable Taylor and Sid Simons. Why, the Natives whispered to each other, does this slander have to be brought up in a public hearing?

"Yes, I heard that rumour," said Constable Taylor.

"And you questioned Redekop about that, didn't you?"

"Yes, I did."

"And did he voluntarily produce for you a sample of his blood?"

"Yes, two samples."

"So were they examined?"

"Yes."

"Did you subsequently interview a Native person who declared that he was the father of the child and no other?"

"Yes."

Rankin had grown increasingly restive during this exchange. He stood up.

"Just so that I might place it on the record," he said, "my friend had interrupted me on the question of relevancy and if there is anything that becomes more remote we are getting into that ground now. We have rumours which my friend sets up and then knocks down. We could go on that exploration forever. I think that in this particular case, I am involved in the issue of the hearing and not some question of paternity. We are not talking about ambush by fatherhood but rather by car. I can't see the relevancy."

"I suppose the relevancy, Mr. Rankin, was that of animosity," said the coroner, taking a hand in the discussion. "This would certainly be indicative of that type of question. I happen to have the report here." He paused. "By the way, we are talking about the Charlie Chaplin case really. The blood was checked and we proved the positive and not the negative . . . you know. . . . "

Simons had a correction. "It was only Marlon Brando that was able to prove . . . "

"Was it Marlon Brando?" queried the coroner. He turned to Harry Rankin who was twisting impatiently in his chair. "I quite agree with you, Mr. Rankin, that we are not going to ask the real father to stand up."

"I don't intend to pursue the point," said Simons.

"I think you made your point on animosity," the coroner replied.

The locals facing the coroner were bemused. Said one, "Hot damn! I never thought I'd hear about the sex lives of Charlie Chaplin and Marlon Brando in a Vanderhoof courtoom!"

SID SIMONS MOVED INTO AN AREA which had had much media attention.

"Some of the people told you that Coreen Thomas was playing chicken on the roadway?"

"Yes."

"I am going to play dumb, Mr. Simons," interjected the coroner. "What is 'playing chicken' or 'playing rooster' or whatever it is on the highway?"

Taylor explained: "Playing chicken in this particular area as I gathered from witnesses at the scene is that a person hitchhiking along the road observes a vehicle coming and in an attempt to make the vehicle stop, will walk out—wander out into the middle of the road or onto the travelled portion of the road to see whether or not the vehicle will stop. Whatever occurs thereafter—if the vehicle does not stop or the person does not get hit—one way or another the car will proceed on."

"Thank you," said the coroner.

As Simons' questioning continued, Taylor asserted that when he was questioning Richard Redekop in the early morning hours of July 3, he knew that he was investigating an accident in which charges might be laid and that from time to time, he raised his voice—he got "heavy," to quote Simons.

The constable went on to explain that he also got "heavy" with Redekop's companion, Faye Haugen. She wanted to take her child home to bed; the constable insisted on questioning her. "I thought at the time that it was necessary to obtain a statement from Miss Haugen and she was reluctant to give me one. I considered charges of obstruction at that time."

"When you said that you might keep her in overnight is when Mr. Redekop said he was going to phone a lawyer?"

"Yes."

"And you said she could go home, he didn't have to phone a lawyer about it and they were both permitted to leave?"

"That is correct."

Towards the end of Simons' questioning, he asked, "Did you threaten any person that you were interviewing, either physically or in any manner to require them to say certain things?"

"No."

Sid Simons sat down.

AN OUT-OF-TOWNER, A MEMBER of the group some citizens of Vanderhoof resented, stepped outside to stretch his legs. He walked towards the main street. As he looked around he thought that Vanderhoof had not changed since his last visit a few years before. The streets were still caked with mud from passing pickup trucks and the buildings had a rundown look about them. An air of stagnation, he thought, that's what I feel here. The air of stagnation and the overtones of racism he was picking up at the inquest left him depressed. He had come to the inquest out of an interest in race relations. Now he was vaguely sorry that he had come.

When he returned to the auditorium, he recognized the wiry figure of Bishop Remi De Roo near the coffee urn, deep in conversation with a Native elder. For some reason the sight of those two walking together tempered his feeling of melancholy and he moved back to the hearing room with a lighter step.

MURRAY MILLER, COUNSEL for the Thomas family, jackknifed out of his chair and leaned over the papers before him. As he stood up more than one spectator wondered what on earth was left for Taylor to answer. It developed that, indeed, there was still a point or two to cover. Miller questioned the interrogations of the young Native witnesses. He established with Constable Taylor that the younger ones were interviewed individually, with just himself and a witness in the room.

"Did it ever occur to you that they should have had adults present when they were being questioned?"

"The adults were not present at the accident scene," said the constable, "so I did not see what they could add to it. . . . I wasn't taking statements from these witnesses with the intention of charging them with an offence under the Juvenile Deliquent's Act. They were solely witnesses to the accident."

The constable admitted that some of the witnesses appeared nervous, especially Coreen's sister Marjorie. He said that she was crying.

"And did you stop questioning her when she cried?"

"Yes, I let her cry."

Close to the front Coreen's father moved uneasily in his seat as he listened to the words of the constable. He thought of little Margie crying with no one to comfort her but this stern-faced man. The picture of his timid young daughter hurt him. He felt his eyes stinging.

"And then what did you do?" asked Miller.

"Talked to her."

"You continued to question her?"

"That's correct."

Constable Taylor denied that he accused Marjorie of lying. "I told her to tell the truth."

"Then you said, 'Isn't it a fact that Coreen was playing chicken?'"

"I may have asked if Coreen was playing chicken or what she knew about playing chicken or whether she heard Coreen say that she was playing chicken."

BRIDGET MORAN

"Isn't it a fact that she denied it at first?"

"She may have, yes."

"And you persisted in this questioning and she finally came around to your way of thinking?"

"I don't believe so."

Miller moved into the area of the uttering of threats by Constable Taylor. "You said that you never threatened anyone, but you also said you were going to hold Faye Haugen unless she made a statement—that is a threat."

The constable did not see that as a threat.

Sid Simons stood up. "I wonder if my friend would be kind enough to allow me to look after the interests of that person?"

"I was wondering if he was looking after everyone's interests," interjected the coroner. "I understand who you do represent, but we have a long way to go."

Harry Rankin rose from his chair. "May I make an observation?"

"You probably will," said the coroner ruefully.

"First of all," said Rankin, "Mr. Simons is not in a position to decide who should be looked after. The question of a threat can take many forms. My friend Mr. Simons elicited a question of how Faye Haugen was treated for the purpose of showing that this police officer was firm and treated the white witnesses the same as the Indian witnesses. Then he went on to say and elicited from the officer that there were no threats to any witnesses. To say to a person with a little child, 'I may hold you overnight,' can be construed as a threat, especially if it is a jail you are going to. That is what Mr. Miller is talking about, and I submit that it is a proper question, except that my friend Mr. Simons is using it to show how fair this situation was, and my other friend, Mr. Miller, is using it to show that when the constable wanted to, he used threats, either implied or direct, and in my submission that is squarely the issue we are talking about."

"Miss Haugen is present and she will testify and you can ask her directly whether she considered that to be a threat or not," said the coroner.

Rankin was not finished. "But she now has an interest in not being threatened, and the constable is the witness that is in the box."

"With the greatest conceivable respect," interjected Simons, "she has an interest in telling the truth in court."

"She also has an interest in protecting her husband," said Rankin, "and that is a common sense position. Anyone knows that."

"I agree," said the coroner. He looked slightly befuddled. "Well, you are both doing the talking." Turning to Miller, he asked, "What did you want to do?"

Rankin was not sitting down. "I am entitled to make objections because I am going to be dealing with this question."

The coroner turned again to Miller. "Would you just go ahead with whether it was a threat or not a threat? The witness doesn't know whether it was a threat, he's just a policeman in a uniform."

Miller elicited information from the constable that he had not said to anyone that he would hold that person in custody or lay a charge of obstruction. Neither had Taylor questioned Redekop as to whether or not Coreen was playing chicken that fatal morning.

AS MILLER SAT DOWN the coroner indicated that he wished to ask some general questions.

"The City Fathers and the aldermen of Vanderhoof," he noted, "in their wisdom decided to have a celebration. They decided to have a street dance and therefore they did some advertising—'Everybody come to town and have a ball!' Was there any requirement that you have an extra force on duty that night?"

"No," answered the constable. He estimated that there were between two hundred and fifty and three hundred people dancing in the street that night. He said that he was the Chief Constable that night.

"Now," asked the coroner, "how were the people to get home from this great celebration when they have to go seven or eight or nine miles back to the reservation? Was there any transportation laid on? . . . Was a woman just four days off her term of pregnancy to walk nine or seven miles? The City Fathers didn't consider that aspect? They were just to pour home after the street dancing was over and go seven or eight or nine miles?"

"Yes," said the constable, "or find suitable transportation to arrive at their homes."

And the coroner wondered about those faceless readers who read Taylor's reports in Prince George—who were they? Did they communicate with anyone, perhaps even Coroner Turner?

"I have no knowledge," said the constable. "I supplied Coroner Turner with my investigation of the accident and it was his decision to have an inquest or inquiry."

"Not yours?"

"Not mine."

The coroner nodded. Constable Taylor left the stand.

BY MID-AFTERNOON ON THE first day of the inquest a study in contrasts had developed in the high school. On the one hand there was the structured, rather formal atmosphere in the gymnasium where the inquest was ongoing. On the other hand there was the freewheeling, distinctly social air just beyond the gymnasium's doors. The women selling coffee had a familiar greeting for nearly everyone they served, farmers and ranchers hailed the townspeople, young Natives lounged in the sunshine that filtered in near the door. Constables paced the floor, stopping now and then to greet an acquaintance or to warn a group of

JUDGEMENT AT STONEY CREEK

teenagers to quiet down. Reporters prowled the hallway, their
tape recorders and cameras at the ready. While white Vanderhoof teenagers kept well away from the group of young Indians,
many older whites and Natives could be seen talking together.

Just outside the gymnasium a young reporter questioned a
middle-aged white man. He said that he thought the inquest was
more of a trial than anything else. "There's been more than one
person on trial than the driver of the car that killed Coreen
Thomas," he added. "I would also say the townspeople of
Vanderhoof have been on trial, the coroner, the RCMP and
possibly in an overall way, the federal Department of Indian
Affairs and their policies. The reporting has been unfair, it's been
long-distance reporting, not reporting from reporters who have
been here long enough to get a feel of what the town is like and
the problems we have here. I would say the press has been, in
some cases, irresponsible."

Nearby a Native courtworker was emphasizing quite a different point of view with another reporter. "The fact is that more
young Natives go to jail each year than graduate from high
school. We are under ten percent of the population, and yet if
you visited a jail, say in Prince George, you would find between
sixty and seventy percent of the inmates are Indian. Why? We
are not more criminal than the white people. Statistics show that
when it comes to violent crimes we might even be less criminal.
So why do we fill the jails and the reform schools? I believe that
this inquest is uncovering one big reason—we have two justice
systems here in Vanderhoof, and across Canada—if it comes to
that—a white justice system and a Native justice system. In my
work in courtrooms I see these two systems in action all the
time."

10

A LTHOUGH IT WAS ONLY mid-afternoon when Constable Taylor left the witness stand to be replaced by Dr. Jim
Swanney, there was a feeling that already the day had been very
long.

In a fine Scots accent, Dr. Swanney stated that he had qualified as a physician at the University of Glasgow, obtained a
Diploma in Medical Jurisprudence in London in 1972, and had
experience in Forensic Medicine at the University of Glasgow
and as a Deputy Police Surgeon in that same city. He was, he
said, a practicing physician in the neighbouring town of Fraser
Lake. He stated that he performed the autopsy after Coreen's
death.

Harry Rankin stood up. He wished to ensure, he said, that
the doctor did not deal in forensic medicine.

"He will offer some small opinion," said Macarthur.

"I certainly would agree that his qualifications are acceptable
if Your Honour will accept them," said Sid Simons, "especially
since he is from the same place [as the coroner]."

"I find that helpful," said the coroner with a smile.

Rankin cut through this bit of legalese banter. "I thought we
are all supposed to have come from the same place," he said
shortly.

Cliff Macarthur noted that Dr. Swanney examined the body,
and subsequently performed the autopsy. "Could you," he asked,
"tell us the extent of your examination, the observations you
made, and your conclusions, if any?"

Coreen, said the doctor, was an obviously pregnant girl. He had found massive grazing and abrasions to her back, hands, and feet, and a massive bruise over the back of her head. He found, upon opening the body, a normally developed male fetus. He concluded, he said, that the primary cause of death was a hemorrhage into the brain. "I made the observation," he said, "that the body appeared to have been dragged for some distance following the impact, but that the impact did not appear to have been that of a high speed accident."

Asked to clarify this, he stated that in high speed accidents, ones in which a body is hit by a vehicle travelling at a high speed at the moment of impact, one normally finds the long bones and/or the spinal column broken. Coreen's body looked to him, he said, as if it had been pushed rather than thrown. "This is very much simplifying it," he added. "Obviously this has to be tied in with other evidence . . . the car could have been travelling quite quickly but braked some distance before it hit the girl, and the speed of impact might have been quite slow." He thought that death occurred a very few minutes after the injuries.

"How long does a fetus live in the body after the death of the mother?" asked Macarthur.

"I feel that once the maternal blood supply is cut off you have four or five minutes when you do something with the fetus."

"That's all?"

"It is worthwhile doing it up to ten minutes, but after that there is no point."

Sophie Thomas sat, her head in her hands, as the doctor continued to give his evidence. It was almost more than she could bear to listen to his words, and to relate them to the pretty laughing Coreen who had treated her aunt's house like a second home all of her young life.

Dr. Swanney confirmed that he had taken a blood sample from the body two days after the accident to test for alcohol content. The blood sample had been given to Constable Davis. The delay of two days would not materially alter the level of alcohol in the blood, he said, since the body had been in a refrigerated state.

RANKIN, AND AFTER HIM SID SIMONS, tested a number of possibilities which would account for the injuries to Coreen's body—a car going sixty miles an hour hits the brakes and slows to thirty before hitting a person; a person thrown on to the hood of a car, carried along and then flung off when the brakes are applied; a person being struck not at high speed by a vehicle but having been caught in some manner by clothing or by a fender and then dragged forward as the car proceeded. Yes, said the doctor, any one of these is a possibility.

Murray Miller questioned Coreen's blood alcohol count.

"When the body was brought to you," he asked, "did you notice any alcohol smell?"

"No, I didn't," answered the doctor. "In fact I commented thereon to the constable—that there was no smell of alcohol from the body. Normally one would expect to smell alcohol, especially when you open the body. I did receive a report that there was alcohol present in the body."

The coroner interjected that there would be testimony during the inquest that Coreen's blood sample had an alcohol reading of .19. "Does that change any answers you gave to learned counsel here?"

"Not really," answered the doctor. "I didn't smell alcohol."

The coroner wasn't quite finished. With the names of Charlie Chaplin and Marlon Brando dancing around in his head, the doctor seemed to him a likely person to answer questions about the establishment of paternity. "I am going where angels fear to tread," said Glen MacDonald. "Is it possible to prove that a person is the father of a child, or can you only prove a negative, that he is not the father?" The doctor responded with statistics about Rhesus groupings, positive and negative antibodies, matching pairs. Pencils at the press table stopped moving and spectators shuffled their feet, but the doctor and the coroner appeared oblivious to the general air of befuddlement around them.

The examination of Dr. Swanney finished with a round of questions and answers about the connection between pregnancy and alcohol. Women, he said, seemed to get just as drunk whether or not they were pregnant.

"But no drunker?" queried Miller.

"I would say no drunker," replied the doctor.

A FRESH-FACED YOUNG CONSTABLE followed the doctor into the stand.

Brian Craig Reed, in the RCMP for approximately two years, told Cliff Macarthur that he was in the vehicle that picked up Richard Redekop after the accident. He checked Coreen for signs of life, made markings of the position of her body on the road, accompanied Redekop to the police station and read to him the demand for a breathalyser test, and went to the Vanderhoof Hospital at 5 a.m. to find out who had pronounced death.

"When I arrived at the hospital I learned that in fact no one had yet pronounced death." He requested the presence of a doctor, he said, and at 5:25 a.m. Dr. Stephen pronounced Coreen dead in the hospital morgue.

He stated that he subsequently interviewed a number of witnesses, including Faye Haugen, and that he received blood samples from Coreen's body and forwarded them to the City Analyst Laboratory in Vancouver.

11

THE FOG WAS FIGHTING a losing battle with autumnal sunshine when the inquest reconvened on the morning of September 26. Because the day was Sunday, a traditional day of leisure even in the farming community of Vanderhoof, the gymnasium filled rapidly. The division of the crowd, so noticeable the day before, was still evident—Natives near the back of the room, white spectators closer to the lawyers and the coroner's table. Breaking this pattern, Sophie Thomas, Mary John, Mary's daughter Helen Jones, and Coreen's parents Matilda and Peter Thomas, sat in the third row. Periodically Sophie Thomas cupped her ear with a hand in a vain effort to overcome the echoing vastness of the gymnasium's ceiling.

On this Sunday morning, the ladies of the piano fund had many requests for strong black coffee. Their best customers, they said, came from the press table.

SERGEANT JOSEPH RENE EDWARD D'Aoust was still under oath and was in the witness stand when proceedings opened. Before questioning of him could begin again a juror indicated that he wished to speak. "Your Honour, the jury requests that Dr. Stephen appear on the witness stand." Mr. Macarthur replied, "We will look after that, yes."

After Sid Simons covered a few points, Murray Miller stood up. He asked if he was correct in believing that the sergeant's findings were that at minimum, the Redekop vehicle had been travelling between 37.02 and 41.18 miles per hour at the start of the skid which ended with Coreen being struck.

"That is correct."

"And you stated that you have no idea what the maximum was; it could have been considerably more?"

"Yes, it could have been considerably more."

"I have no further questions," said Mr. Miller.

A juror indicated that he wished to question Sergeant D'Aoust.

"Yes, Mr. Juror?" said the coroner.

Why, asked the juror, were there four skid marks and not the conventional two which would be expected from a car that was under control?

The sergeant replied that four skid marks are very common. Also common are two skid marks where the wheels have over-lapped; the number of skid marks, he said, does not necessarily indicate whether or not a vehicle is under control. He went on to instruct the jurors and the coroner on what makes skid marks. "A tire mark," he said, "what is commonly known as a tire mark . . . is not the tire, the rubber on the pavement, it's the melting of the tar that lifts out of the pavement causing the black marks."

After some discussion with the coroner about the differences to be found between asphalt and concrete and the effect on skid marks of the number of people in a vehicle, Sergeant D'Aoust was excused.

"I understand he wants to get back to his detachment," said Macarthur.

Macarthur had some information about Dr. Stephen. "He is apparently in the country somewhere branding cattle. He will be here in an hour and a half."

"Jesus!" said a reporter. "These doctors are sure jacks of all trade!"

"The next witness will be James Morris," continued Macarthur, "whose evidence will be led by my friend, Mr. W.R. Stephen, who is appearing with me."

AS THE YOUNGISH BEARDED MAN took the stand, the people near Sophie Thomas visibly relaxed. He was a white man with whom many of the Natives in the gymnasium were acquainted—they felt a trust in him and his evidence that expressed itself in nods and whispered asides among themselves.

He identified himself as James Hay Morris, residing at the corner of 6th Street and Nechako Avenue (Kenney Dam Road) where he was living on July 3. His home, he said, was fifteen or twenty feet from the spot where Coreen died.

"There were a number of people hitchhiking on the road," he continued, "and our bedroom overlooks the road. I was laying partially awake hearing voices drifting up. At approximately ten to three or five to three in the morning, I heard the sound of an impact, followed by a car halting. . . . I heard the sound of tires and the sound of gravel followed by silence, and then people started to yell. At that point I was looking out the window and people were yelling, 'You won't get away with that' and statements of that sort."

Coreen's father put his head in his hands. "Oh God!" he moaned quietly to himself.

After a pause Morris went on. "I saw people running up the hill just past 6th Street. There was a large dark car slightly above 6th Street which backed down on to 6th Street and went down the hill. People were making a lot of noise outside, and I tried to holler down as to whether they needed help, assistance in the form of an ambulance or police. It took a couple of minutes to get through to them because there was a lot of noise and commotion, and finally we did manage to talk to someone down

JUDGEMENT AT STONEY CREEK

there. They said yes, they did require police and an ambulance, so I went to the phone and phoned first the police and then the hospital for the ambulance."

Following the phone calls he found a flashlight and went down to the road. Using his flashlight, he checked Coreen for vital signs. "I couldn't find any pulse," Morris said. "I just listened for respiration. I didn't find any."

Within a few minutes another car drove up and the driver checked Coreen for signs of life. "Then," said Morris, "we simply stood and directed traffic and waited for the police or the ambulance to arrive."

"And did they?" asked Mr. Stephen.

"After a considerable delay," replied Morris.

He estimated that the police arrived about 3:30. On arrival, he said, the police checked the girl: "One of the officers borrowed my flashlight and . . . checked her eyes and checked for pulse. At that point I asked my wife to bring down a blanket, and once the police were satisfied, they covered the girl."

Morris stated that the ambulance arrived forty-five or fifty minutes after he heard the impact.

IN HIS QUESTIONING HARRY Rankin zeroed in on sounds. "What kind of an impact was that in terms of sound? I know that is difficult to describe, but if you would?"

"It was a crushing noise," said Morris. "The impact only meant one thing. The moment I sat up I told my wife that somebody had been hit . . . it wasn't a clear sound, it was involved in braking and there was quite a bit of gravel kicked around that corner from 6th Street out, and the car was probably riding on gravel to a certain extent. There were certainly tire sounds involved as well."

Sid Simons, in his examination, had other concerns.

"Were you able to judge," he asked, "whether the persons on the roadway when you first went out appeared to be sober or otherwise?"

"There were no obvious signs of people drinking," the witness replied, "but it was possible because of the accident . . . but the people that were there were greatly distressed because of the accident, in the case of the girl's sister, or else were standing very quietly around the girl. I talked to a couple of people afterwards. One was Mr. Raphael, and at the time he appeared to be quite sober."

Morris confirmed that he heard no sounds of argument, no name-calling, until after the accident.

Murray Miller was interested in one of Morris' last statements.

He remembered that in his evidence of the day before, Constable Taylor in describing Cecil Raphael at the scene of the accident had said, "I would have arrested this person for being intoxicated in a public place. His speech was quite slurred. I could not understand him when he told me his name." "Just to clear up a point," Miller now asked, "did you say you were talking to Cecil Raphael?"

"Yes, sir, I believe it was Cecil, if he's the taller fellow, moustache, dark longer hair?"

"And you say he seemed sober?"

James Morris assured the lawyer that he talked to Raphael and that he seemed completely sober.

"Did you talk to anyone else [at the scene]?"

"Just very briefly to other people that were on the—right on the scene."

"And they seemed sober?"

The prosecutor, Mr. Stephen, interjected. "Mr. Morris, did you know Cecil Raphael beforehand?"

"No, I did not."

"So you can't positively state that the person you spoke to was Cecil Raphael?"

"The easiest thing in the world is to bring Cecil Raphael in to show him," said Rankin.

"Is he present?" asked the coroner. "I don't mind."

Cecil Raphael was brought in from the nether regions to which witnesses had been banished. When Morris confirmed that this was the person he had spoken to on the night of the accident, many of the Natives in the audience smiled. "So much for Taylor's evidence," muttered Raphael's cousin to his neighbour.

"Thank you," said the coroner. "I think that's the point."

Before Morris left the stand, the coroner wanted answers to a few questions. In an effort to find out how long it took Morris to leave his house and arrive at the scene of the accident, the coroner asked, "Do you sleep in pajamas?"

"No, sir."

Was Morris putting on his clothes at the time that people were yelling "You won't get away with this!" and "You killed her!"? "Don't be backward now," said the coroner. "If there is anything else that was shouted or yelled, or swearing, we don't mind hearing it, just give it to us."

"There was considerable commotion, but people were yelling, it was my feeling at least that it was directed towards the driver for hitting the girl."

"When you looked at Coreen, do you recall the colour of her clothing?"

"I believe dark-coloured clothing, possibly a brown blouse. She was wearing slacks, they could have been dark-coloured again."

The coroner had one more question. "When you looked out in your nude condition, did you have any difficulty identifying people?"

"Well," said Morris, "I would have had difficulty if I had to tell who they were, yes."

"That's all I have, unless you've got any questions, Mr. Foreman, or jurors? Thank you for helping us. You may be excused if you wish."

James Hay Morris stepped down.

A TALL BESPECTACLED MAN, Glen Clark, moved into the witness stand. He identified himself as editor of the *Nechako Chronicle* and volunteer emergency ambulance driver and attendant.

Bishop Remi De Roo was interested in Clark and the evidence he was about to give. The bishop had visited with this newspaperman one evening and was later to write about his visit in his report as Chairperson of the Human Rights Commission of British Columbia: "Glen Clark was formerly postmaster and recalled seeing the Post Office befouled by Indian people drinking and otherwise messing up the premises after hours. He went on at length about the harassment of whites by Native people who drink and then cause scenes in local shops and public places. . . . He said he was trying very hard to remain calm and objective but then felt with the majority of the population that things had gone too far." Despite this damning of the aboriginal group by the editor of the *Nechako Chronicle*, the bishop's report echoed a hope that Clark could somehow be a partner in improving the racial climate in Vanderhoof.

Led by Macarthur's assistant, Mr. Stephen, Glen Clark's evidence concerned not his ethnic views, but his work as a volunteer ambulance attendant. He stated that Vanderhoof had two emergency ambulance crews and that his crew was on duty during the early morning hours of July 3, 1976. Clark said that when an emergency requiring ambulance services occurs, Vanderhoof citizens call the hospital. The hospital, he said, takes the message as to the location of the emergency and immediately hospital personnel press a button on a radio control system which beeps a pager carried by a member of the ambulance crew on duty. The person paged then phones the hospital to find out where the emergency service is required.

Clark testified that his beeper went off at 3:30 a.m. on the morning of July 3. "Once the beeper had gone," he said, "I sprang from my bed and went to the telephone, phoned the hospital, told them I was responding and requested information as to where or what the problem was."

He estimated that five minutes after the beeper awakened him, he arrived at the firehall where the ambulance was ready to go. The attendant accompanying him had already been instructed by the hospital to proceed to Kenney Dam Road and 6th Street. Clark further estimated that only another two or three minutes elapsed before the ambulance reached the scene of the accident.

Arriving there, he said, he checked whether anything could be done for the victim. "There was no pulse. There was no breathing," he said. "After that my driver, myself, with some assistance, loaded the person onto a stretcher, and we put her into the ambulance and conveyed her to the hospital."

"And what time did you arrive at the hospital?" asked Mr. Stephen.

"I arrived at the hospital at 4 a.m. . . . we unloaded the stretcher containing the victim and took her into the emergency ward of the hospital, where we were met by a nurse, and the nurse immediately tested again for signs of life, and at that point we, on her direction, took the person on the stetcher to the morgue in the hospital."

"And is that normal procedure, Mr. Clark?" asked the prosecutor.

"It's not quite normal. Normally there's a doctor to pronounce death. . . . There was no doctor present at that particular time."

"So you took the body to the morgue. What did you do next?"

"Unloaded the body from the stretcher to a morgue slab, and the body was placed into the cooler of the morgue."

"Thank you," said Mr. Stephen. "That's all I have. Would you answer any other questions, please?"

WHILE MR. CLARK HAD BEEN giving his evidence, several copies of the editorial he had written a few days before, eulogizing Vanderhoof coroner Eric Turner and headlined "Service Above Self," had arrived as if by magic on the lawyers' table. Harry Rankin stood up, every muscle of his body expressing outrage.

"Mr. Coroner," he said angrily, "there are a lot of papers going back and forth on this table. Now this gentleman, besides being the ambulance driver, apparently is the editor of the paper as well. It is not my intention to go into this garbage"—Rankin picked up a copy of the editorial and dropped it—"but if my friends are going to bring it up, then I will deal with it too." He asked the coroner to rule on the admissability of the editorial. "It would seem to me," Rankin continued, "it would clutter up the inquest and do no good, so I just want that objection. I don't know how Your Honour wants to treat it."

"No," said the coroner, "I just want to hear about his duties as an ambulance attendant." Turning to the witness, he asked, "You don't particularly want to give us the editorial, do you?"

"No, sir," said Clark.

Sid Simons was on his feet. He pointed out that the witness had brought the material to the inquest. "Perhaps," he said, "the witness would like to do something with it." Could the witness be excused and perhaps recalled later when the papers have been examined? "That might assist, it might assist in shortening this. . . . "

"I would not think it would assist anybody," interrupted Rankin.

The Coroner cut the discussion short. "I will make my ruling now. As far as I'm concerned the ambulance records, Exhibit 11, is all I want from this witness. If anybody wants to buy a paper, they can go out on the street and buy their own."

Having made his ruling on the editorial, the coroner had a question or two of the witness.

"How is it," he asked, "that you've got a doctor on call, and yet we don't have a doctor and in fact we have no medical certification of death? Was there any mouth-to-mouth resuscitation done by anyone, or was this just an on-the-spot assessment of death and that was it?"

"As I said to Your Honour," answered Clark, "when I arrived on the scene there was a blanket and sheet pulled over the victim, and there was no mouth-to-mouth resuscitation done prior to my arrival. There was none done by myself."

The coroner was not satisfied. "Well, I'm not going into the requirements of first aid treatment, but it seems almost casual that now we get to the hospital and there is still no medical certification of death and somebody has her locked in the morgue."

"That is correct," Clark replied. "I was disturbed myself at this in particular—but I was told that the doctor was coming and that he would pronounce death, and once we arrive at the hospital it's up to the hospital administration to make decisions."

A juror had other concerns.

"A former witness has told us that the hospital was phoned at three in the morning. Can you give us any reason why it should take forty minutes for your beeper to be set off?"

Clark shook his head. "I have absolutely no idea why there should be such a discrepancy. It's approximately a five-foot walk from the telephone in the hospital to the button which pushes the beeper. I only know that when the beeper goes off, it's our job to respond and to respond immediately, which we do."

Clark left the stand.

The coroner looked at his watch. "I think we will give the reporters' hands a rest. Can we be back here," he asked, "at, say, a quarter to eleven?"

ONCE AGAIN VANDERHOOF was basking in late morning sunshine. Outside the high school a Band Councillor from Stoney Creek was discussing a statement circulating at the inquest that seventy percent of the adults on her reserve had problems with alcohol. "I don't think that stuff like that should be said, because alcohol is a problem in every society, not just Indians. There are alcoholics in all walks of life," she continued, "right down to doctors and lawyers and whatever. Indians are more open about it, they go and drink on the street. I think that's the reason they say only Indians are alcoholic and what not. I think there are lots of things you don't know and I don't know, I bet, but Indians drink and they don't hide it. They go to the bar and have a good time."

She laughed. "I like to go to the bar myself once in a while and have a good time. It's not the problem of Indians only. Alcohol is a problem for everybody."

12

REPORTERS CLUSTERED in a group outside the gymna-sium in the brilliant September sunshine.

"Who is next on the witness stand?" asked one.

"The constable who gave the breathalyser test," answered another, his British accent very much in evidence, "and then I gather there is an expert, a bird from Vancouver—she's the last word on breathalyser tests."

"Oh, hell!" said the first reporter. "Any bets about how soon we'll get some more non-information on oxidation?"

"I don't mind that," said another reporter. "It's that frigging coefficient of friction that drives me around the bend!"

CONSTABLE DONALD DAVIS identified himself as a member of the RCMP, Vanderhoof detachment, with over four years service in the force. He had, he said, specialized training in the operation of the breathalyser machine and was a desig-nated technician of the machine under the Criminal Code of Canada.

On the morning of July 3 he had administered two breatha-lyser tests to Richard Redekop, the first sample being taken at 4:22 a.m. with a reading of .08, and the second at 4:36 a.m. with a reading of .05. Mr. Redekop, he added, appeared to be quite sober. "The only symptoms that would indicate any impair-ment," he said, "was his eyes were slightly bloodshot."

On July 5, Constable Davis said, he was present when Dr. Swanney performed an autopsy on Coreen Thomas. In the process a blood sample was taken and handed to Constable Davis, who turned the sample over to Constable Reed.

Almost immediately Harry Rankin moved into the dreaded area of oxidation.

"Assuming that the accident occurred at 3:05 and the person that you registered on the machine was the same person, they would have approximately .015 on top of the .08 reading, is that correct? In other words, if your reading was taken at 3:05 in the morning instead of 4:22 . . . they would have a higher reading?"

"That's correct," said the constable.

"And that higher reading would be .08 plus the .015, is that correct?"

"That is also dependent on when the person had his last drink."

"Yes, that's right," agreed Rankin, "but that [.08 plus .015] would be an approximation?"

"It could be higher, I can say that. . . . "

Rankin moved into the area of "bloodshot eyes." Observing this, he asked, did the constable perform any tests for sobriety—finger-to-nose, heel-to-toe, picking up coins? No, said the officer, he was off shift that night and was only called in to do a breathalyser test.

Many young drivers in the high school gymnasium, Native and non-Native, listened with more than a touch of cynicism to this casual testing of Redekop's sobriety. They recalled being hauled out of their vehicles, often in the dark of night, shoved and pushed and ordered in a loud and threatening voice, "Touch your nose with your finger! Pick up that money! Do this! Do that!" Man, oh man! thought these young people, it never before stopped a cop, just because he was off-duty, from man-handling us!

SID SIMONS WAS INTERESTED in other areas.

"Have you," he asked the constable, "investigated any other

fatal vehicle accidents recently?"

Yes, said the constable. He affirmed that he had investigated a fatal accident about five miles along Kenney Dam Road in January or February of 1976, in which the deceased was a Native as was the driver of the accident vehicle. He confirmed that no charges had been laid. He went on, in answer to further questions from Sid Simons, to state that he had also investigated the accident in which Bonnie Redekop, Richard Redekop's sister, had subsequently lost her life. . . .

The coroner interrupted the questioning. "I was only sent up here to do an inquest on one person. Unless there is some relevance to this, we can go back ten, twenty years." He appealed to Simons. "Just help me. Where are you going with these other people who have died? I don't want to confuse my foreman and jurors. . . ."

"Your Honour," replied Simons, "I am attempting as briefly as possible to deal with certain suggestions or implications that seem to be arising from some cross-examination of some of the witnesses." His intention, he said, was to show that individuals and families on both sides of Coreen's death were relevant considerations—Natives kill Natives and are not charged, a white girl dies in a vehicle accident and again no charges are laid.

"Thank you," said the coroner. "I just wanted you to explain to me where you were going. I understand now."

MURRAY MILLER WAS CONCERNED with the discrepancy in the first and second readings of Redekop's breathalyser tests.

"The breathalyser reading was .03 lower in the space of fourteen minutes or so. Is that unusual?"

"Yes," replied the constable.

"What would cause that?"

"A poor sample, a poor breath sample would cause the low reading."

"So the .05 was a poor sample, is that correct?"

"I didn't think so at the time. . . . It's possible it was a poor sample."

What, asked the coroner, would cause a poor sample?

"When a person blows into the breathalyser," answered the constable, "we're after the last one-third of his breath, deep lung air."

"So that is your explanation as to why the reading dropped from eight to five?"

The constable nodded. "Yes, I would say it's not the deep lung air."

More than one of the reporters grinned—an old trick employed by Redekop, they thought, and the cop didn't catch it!

FOLLOWING CONSTABLE DAVIS onto the stand was Dr. Charles Stephen, a small balding man just in, presumably, after branding cattle. He was questioned by W.R. Stephen, acting with Cliff Macarthur.

"Dr. Stephen questioned by Mr. Stephen," muttered a reporter. "I hope I can keep these Stephens straight!"

The doctor had a rather embarrassed air as he related the events of the early morning hours of July 3. He had several acquaintances, friends, and patients in the gymnasium. Sensing his discomfort, many of them smiled as he took the stand.

"Sometime on the morning of July 3rd," he began, "I was called from the hospital to say that a body had arrived and would I come over and pronounce it dead and I said I would. . . . "

"Do you know what time this was?"

"I don't know what time it was, no. I had no watch available with me when I was sleeping."

"And what happened?"

"I fell asleep, and a second phone call was made saying that Constable Reed was there and would like me to come and view the body with him."

"What time was this?"

"That was approximately five o'clock, I would think."

Dr. Stephen described his examination of Coreen's body, including the information that her body temperature was below thirty-two degrees centigrade. ("No bloody wonder!" muttered Rankin's son-in-law to Rankin. "She had been in that cooler for over an hour!")

"I pointed out to the constable," said Dr. Stephen, "that more significant in determining the time of death was to indicate to him that the patient probably died very suddenly because there were rather marked abrasions over the back of her hands and on the front of her shins and feet and there was no blood coming from these, indicating the the patient was in a state of death or profound shock almost immediately."

A juror had some questions.

"We were told that when Coreen Thomas was taken to the hospital, the ambulance drivers were instructed to place her in the morgue before a doctor arrived, and that this is not usual procedure. I am wondering if you can tell us about that."

"No," replied the doctor, "it is not entirely usual procedure. In general, we will see the patient in the out-patient department and pronounce the person dead there. That is really the correct way to do things. In the early hours of the morning we have one nurse on duty and so there's help needed in transferring the patient, and when patients are brought in dead—the ambulance drivers are really helping the nurse to take the body upstairs and they are really assuming that the patient is dead at the time; that is correct."

"As I understand it," the juror persisted, "isn't the only person who is qualified to pronounce a person dead is a medical doctor?"

"That is correct," said the doctor.

Mary John's daughter Helen Jones listened to the evidence

from Dr. Stephen with mounting anger. She had heard it from
Glen Clark, the ambulance attendant, the day before, but somehow Dr. Stephen's measured words had an impact which Clark's
evidence had lacked. Weeks before someone from the hospital
had whispered on the reserve that Coreen had not been pronounced dead before she was wheeled into the morgue. First
Glen Clark and now Dr. Stephen confirmed this. There was no
attempt made, thought Helen, to save Coreen or her baby when
the police and the ambulance attendants found her on the road.
Then to make matters worse she was put in that horrible room
without even a proper medical person making certain that she
was dead. In her anger Helen grouped them all together, the
police, the hospital staff—they don't care how they treat us, she
thought, even when we're dead. Sophie Thomas had said from
the beginning that if Coreen had been white everything would
have been handled in a different way. What Helen had just heard
confirmed every word Sophie had ever said.

Meanwhile the coroner shrugged. "Well, that's the situation,"
he said.

CAROLINE KIRKWOOD, a personable young woman with the
city Analyst Laboratory in Vancouver, followed the doctor into
the witness stand. Questioned by Cliff Macarthur, it was established that she was an instructor in the operation of breathalyser
machines, and that as a chemist with the City Analyst Laboratory, she was responsible for testing Coreen Thomas' blood
sample for alcohol and barbituates. She gave evidence that
Coreen's blood sample gave a blood alcohol reading of .19. No,
she said, the fact that the individual was dead at the time blood
was taken would not affect the reading—the test she administered would accurately indicate the amount of alcohol present
in the blood stream at the time of death.

"Could you tell us, Miss," asked Macarthur, "what meaning, if any, a .19 blood alcohol reading has generally with respect to a person, a female, weighing 140 or 145 pounds?"

"At .19 . . . an individual exhibits the symptoms of intoxication. These can include slurring speech, stumbling gait, inability to choose between alternatives presented towards them such as red and green lights, loss of reaction time, loss of judgement, loss of coordination, tunnel vision, loss of sense of taste, smell, and hearing." In answer to a further question she said that a person having .08 blood alcohol count could have much the same symptoms but perhaps not so pronounced.

Caroline Kirkwood went on to explain that for a 145-pound woman to have a blood alcohol count of .19, and she added that she was speaking generally and making certain assumptions, that woman would have had to consume 7.6 ounces of hard liquor, 5.3 bottles of beer or 21 ounces of wine. A man with a blood alcohol count of .08—Sid Simons interjected to allow that Mr. Redekop weighed 175 pounds—would have consumed 4.7 ounces of hard liquor, 3 bottles of beer or 12 ounces of wine.

Harry Rankin moved into the area of Redekop's breathalyser test results.

"The experienced breathalyser blower—you know, the kind of people who end up in the police station on a number of occasions—sometimes they puff their cheeks out and give a shallow blow. . . . Isn't that's an old trick that sometimes occurs? . . . And some experienced police officers know that they're puffing up their cheeks and not blowing low lung air?"

"That's correct."

"You're the instructor and we'll say in class we've got these two readings [.08 and .05]. What would you say to the officer in a practical way to guide him?"

"I would say take another test until you get good agreement between the two tests," Miss Kirkwood replied. "In other words, I would start again and do another two tests."

SID SIMONS POSED A POSSIBLE explanation of the .03 difference in Richard Redekop's two readings.

"If I were to take a glass, and fill it with a substance," he asked Caroline Kirkwood, "perhaps gin or vodka, and drink it, it would go immediately to my stomach. If I then were to bring up some of the contents of my stomach—if a person is to some degree in shock or demonstrates nausea—and then takes a test on the Borkenstein Breathalyser machine, would the reading be higher, lower, or different than if I had not brought up these stomach contents?"

"If what was brought up from the stomach was alcohol, it could elevate the reading," replied the witness. "It could give a falsely high reading."

Harry Rankin's son-in-law turned to Rankin. "Did Redekop barf before the breathalyser test?" he whispered.

Rankin shrugged. "Who the hell knows!" he muttered.

"And then," continued Simons, "if the person were to calm down in the next ten or fifteen minutes and blow again, the reading would be appreciably lower? The second blow, if you like, would be air from the lungs and not mixed with stomach contents . . . and that could account for the appreciable difference in the two readings?"

"Yes, it may," replied the witness.

In further questioning, Miss Kirkwood said that she did not agree with the physical tests—heel-to-toe, picking up coins—that officers use to test degrees of intoxication. "A police officer, seeing an individual for the first time," she said, "cannot determine whether that individual has an inner ear infection or some other disturbance that prohibits him from performing these tests normally."

"In practical terms," queried Simons, "would you agree that a person with a blood alcohol level of .19 might do something very foolish that that person might not otherwise do if they had not been drinking to that extent?"

"They could, yes."

"And when you speak of their misjudgements to the extent of not being able to tell red from green lights . . . the .19 reading invariably produces that kind of result, does it?"

"Yes."

"Is a person demonstrating that kind of reading likely to be affected by bright lights in the immediate vicinity?"

"Yes. If it's dark and a bright light is shined into the eyes . . . the pupils close automatically. It would lessen the amount of vision that the individual has."

The coroner interrupted. "It's five past twelve. We'll break for lunch and come back, let us say, at 1:40."

As the gymnasium emptied, questions swirled within the Native group about the alcohol level in Coreen's blood. It seemed to be taken as gospel at the inquest, on the basis of the .19 reading, that Coreen had been drunk when she was killed.

"She wasn't drunk," Margie Thomas whispered to her aunt. Donna Patrick nodded. Others in the group around Margie exclaimed, "Coreen wasn't even drinking at the street dance. We were with her!"

If the figure of .19 was right, wondered her family, how was it that the doctor who performed the autopsy had found no smell of alcohol when he, as he put it, "opened her up"? How, they asked helplessly, did so much alcohol get into her blood?

"Maybe," said a cousin hopefully, "we will hear more about it this afternoon."

13

SOON AFTER THE INQUEST reconvened on Sunday afternoon, Cliff Macarthur made a proposal to the coroner and jury.

"We have reached that point," he said, "where we will be dealing with the evidence of eyewitnesses to the accident. My friends and I have discussed a game plan which will hopefully expedite matters. The RCMP took statements from most of the eyewitnesses and the proposal is that we will call them, I will read their statements to them, ask them if that is their statement, and if so then my friends will simply proceed to cross-examine. In that manner it is hoped that all of the circumstances will come out before the jury and that it will expedite matters."

The lawyers agreed as did the coroner who pointed out that, "We can always stop and change the rules, but let's try it this way."

THE FIRST EYEWITNESS to Coreen's death to take the stand was Henry Abe Reddecopp, a dark young man with longish hair and an air of extreme discomfort. Macarthur pointed out that he was no relation to Richard Redekop, whose name was spelled differently.

"I'm going to read your statement," said Macarthur, "and when I'm finished I'm going to ask you if that is your statement. All right? It's headed up, 'This is the statement of Henry Abe Reddecopp born August 3, 1956, of Vanderhoof, B.C., taken by Constable N.A. Taylor, concerning the fatal motor vehicle accident involving Coreen Thomas. There was Shorty (John) Inkster, Mark Cormack and Nick Friemark, and a young Indian girl. We were walking up Stoney Creek Hill on the Kenney Dam Road. There was a bunch of Indian people in front of us. They started calling us names. I was just sitting there by the power pole. Then that's when we met two Indian boys, I think one was Vincent George. We were calling names back and forth for about half an hour.

" 'Then Rick [Richard Redekop], he came up the hill and then as soon as the accident happened he jumped out of the car and Rick said, "Call the police," so I ran down to this house on Fifth Street. I banged on the door and no one answered so I went back up the hill and by this time Rick had already gone down the hill to call the police.

" 'Question: Would you describe what occurred just prior to the accident, where the people were and what they were doing as the vehicle approached? Answer: Aw, I was standing beside the telephone pole. Nick Friemark was on the other side of the road on Sixth Street and Mark Cormack was with me. . . . The Indian girl that got hit was standing just up from Nick Friemark about three feet up from him on the road. The other Indian people were all up further. They all moved up further and off the road when they seen the car coming. The Indian girl that got hit was standing about three inches from the edge of the pavement. Rick was about ten feet or so from her when he put on the brakes and started to skid. Then she ran into the centre of the road in front of Rick's car. I guess then Rick had his brakes locked and she started out in front of him. Then she got hit and she got carried along. . . . Question: How fast was Rick travelling? Answer: I would say about forty-five to fifty miles per hour.' "

Cliff Macarthur lifted his eyes to the witness. "Is that your statement, sir?"

"Yes, it is," said Reddecopp.

"Is it true?"

"Yes."

BEHIND THE WITNESS was a diagram of the accident scene. Harry Rankin asked young Reddecopp to point out the spots where various people were at the precise time when Coreen was hit. Other questions followed.

How far away was the Redekop vehicle when Henry Reddecopp first saw it?

About two blocks, answered the witness, and his speed was about fifty miles an hour.

"All right," said Rankin. "So his speed at Fourth Street was about fifty miles an hour. Did it slacken off at all?"

"Well, he slowed down a bit, and then when he come up here—well, I imagine he kept on the same speed, but—I don't know, there was no change in this."

"There was no change in speed?"

"Not really," answered the witness.

The witness thought that Coreen had been looking down the road and that the right side of the Redekop vehicle caught her. "She was half on the car . . . well, as soon as Rick stopped . . . well, she flew off," said Reddecopp.

"Were you sober that night?" asked Rankin.

"I had a few drinks . . . hard stuff."

The witness said that he had been driving a car for four years.

"Are you able to estimate speeds fairly well?" asked Rankin.

"Not really," said the witness ruefully.

SID SIMONS QUESTIONED Henry Reddecopp about his drinking on the night of the street dance. Henry said he had been drinking hard stuff in a car but that after the dance, as he and his friends walked up the Kenney Dam hill, no one had been drinking or carrying bottles of beer in their hands.

This calling of names—"Was it just somebody calling names like somebody calling Mr. Inkster 'Shorty' and he didn't like being called 'Shorty'?"

"No," said Henry, "there were swear words exchanged . . . [it was] unfriendly."

"There was no fighting, was there? No stand-offs as though people were going to fight?"

"No."

"As far as you were concerned it was nothing serious, it was just people getting at each other?"

"Yeah."

"Was anybody hitchhiking? Was anybody trying to stop cars that were coming along?"

"No," said Reddecopp.

The witness thought that the two groups, Native and white, had been on Kenney Dam hill for about half an hour. He admitted that he might have been mistaken about the time. Did he think he might also have been mistaken about how fast the Redekop vehicle was moving up the hill?

"I might be mistaken at that, too," said Reddecopp.

Before the witness left the stand, the coroner had a request. Would the young man turn to the diagram behind him and write his initials in the spot where he figured he was standing and circle them? "Now, I've marked your statement as Exhibit 14," the coroner said. He then turned to the sheriff and asked him to write a very small number 14 where Coreen was standing before she was hit according to the witness, and another very small 14 at the spot where she ran out to when she was hit. The numbers were entered.

"Now," said the coroner, "I know sometimes this is a bit

theatrical, but would you mind getting up on your feet here and just indicating as best you recall how she moved, how she ran, moved, or whatever she did, from position 14 to position 14 . . . just do the fifteen feet right across in front of counsel, just the same speed, just as it happened."

Henry Reddecopp lurched across the floor in front of the lawyers' table.

"And you saw her do that, did you?" asked the coroner.

"Yes I did," replied the witness.

"She was looking downhill?"

"Yes."

"Thanks very much, Henry."

"You're welcome, sir," replied Reddecopp as he hastened out of the witness stand.

Coreen's father watched numbly as young Reddecopp tried to recreate Coreen's movements in front of the Redekop car. Peter Thomas was afraid that he would break down, make a scene, do something violent, if he had to listen to many more witnesses like this one. It makes it all too real, he thought miserably.

MARK CORMACK, a fifteen-year-old lad, undersized for his age, with fair hair and a bright aspect, followed Reddecopp in the witness stand. His statement, which estimated the Redekop vehicle's speed as between fifty-five and sixty miles per hour, was read. The Indian girl who was hit, Cormack said in his statement, was standing on the pavement on the right side of the road. She came right in front of Redekop's car when she tried to run to the other side of the road. "Then," said the statement, "Rick hit her. She sort of rode along the car as he was stopping. When Rick stopped she flew off the front of the car a few feet."

Questioning by Rankin and Simons drew from him the admission that his only vehicle was a bike, driven on country roads, since he lived out of town. Repeatedly he said that he was not any good at judging distance.

"You don't have experience estimating speeds?" asked Simons.

"No."

"Except on your bike, maybe?"

"Yes."

Once again the witness was asked to indicate on the diagram the spot where he was standing when Coreen was hit, and to re-enact how he remembered Coreen moving in front of the car. Mark had some difficulty with this. "Well, I was like watching the car," he said, "and then she was just there."

Under further questioning from the coroner, Mark thought he had seen about the last four feet of the girl's movement before she was hit—he demonstrated a movement of about four feet that was neither a walk nor a run, but something in between. "It wasn't really like a dash," he said.

"I see," said the coroner. "Thank you very much, Mark. You were good to help us."

WITH THE STATEMENT of the next witness, Peggy Rose Johnny, and her answers during cross-examination, the coroner and the jury heard details of Coreen's movements during the hours preceeding the fatal accident. Peggy, looking much younger than her eighteen years, appeared excessively timid as she answered questions.

She described an afternoon in the hotel room rented by Coreen. There were, she said, four girls in the room—herself, Coreen, Sharon Raphael, and Mildred Thomas. "We were just sitting around watching TV. . . . She [Coreen] bought a case of beer. We drank it all . . . and then we bought two cases before the dance." No, she said, they didn't drink wine or whiskey or anything like that; she thought there was one case of beer left after the dance. She and Sharon had intended to stay in the hotel room with Coreen that night.

"How was it, Peggy," asked Sid Simons, "that you didn't go back up to sleep in the room after the dance?"

"Mildred Thomas was passed out on one bed. . . . Coreen, first she came to me, she said she lost the key so we were looking for it on the ground and couldn't find it, so she went back to the manager and said she wanted to go in her room and asked him for the key and she said she don't have it, she lost it, and she came out, she said they wouldn't let her back in."

"Did you go up and try to wake up Mildred to let you in?"

"They wouldn't let Coreen go up there and wake Mildred up."

"And on that night after the dance and you couldn't get in the hotel room, were you all going to hitchhike out, or how did you figure you were going to get to Stoney Creek?" asked Simons.

"Hitchhike."

"Were you feeling pretty tight yourself?"

"What?"

"Were you feeling kind of tight, you know, drunk a little?"

"No," answered Peggy. "I didn't get drunk that night."

Peggy described the name-calling that went on between the Natives and the non-Natives as the two groups walked up Kenney Dam hill. "Coreen was quarreling with some white guys up there. . . . I went over to meet them and ask them how come they were quarreling with Coreen."

"What do you remember hearing, any swearing going on?"

"Coreen was swearing at them," answered Peggy. "But there was no fighting or pushing, just name-calling. And then, while the quarreling was still going on, the accident happened and Margie [Marjorie] Thomas, Coreen's sister, started screaming at him, the guy who was quarreling with Coreen.

"I just saw her standing there," said Peggy. "I saw her face in

JUDGEMENT AT STONEY CREEK

the lights and I started to run towards her, and the next thing I
knew she was on the ground. . . . Coreen was happy that night.
She had no worries."

Yes, thought Sophie Thomas, Coreen was happy that night,
and she was sober too.

JUST BEFORE THE AFTERNOON coffee break, Lawrence
Johnny, an eighteen-year-old boy from Stoney Creek, was called
to the witness stand. In his statement he said that he was walking
with Donna Patrick up Kenney Dam hill behind Coreen when
he heard a car from towards downtown. "It was coming from
behind us. I turned around and glanced and saw the car go by
me. Then I turned my head forward again and saw the car swerve
towards the left and it went back to the right, and Coreen was
walking on the pavement, and she turned around to look at the
car and she got hit. The car dragged her for fifty feet."

Lawrence estimated that the Redekop vehicle was going
about fifty miles an hour when it struck Coreen. He thought the
car swerved to the left, he said, because "there were some guys
behind Coreen, the car went over this way to go around them."

Like the other witnesses Lawrence put his initials on the
diagram at the spot where he was standing when the vehicle
struck Coreen.

"Was Donna [Patrick] doing any drinking that night or that
afternoon, Lawrence?" asked Sid Simons.

"No."

"None at all, eh?"

"No."

"Okay. Thanks. I've got nothing more, Your Honour."

"Perhaps we can take a coffee break now," said the coroner.

14

S IGNS OF STRAIN were apparent when the inquest resumed at 3:30 on this second day of the Thomas hearing or, to give it its more legalistic title, "An inquisition for the purpose of inquiring into when, where, how and after what manner Coreen Gay Thomas came to her death."

"I can't hear half of what the witnesses are saying," muttered David Stone to his father-in-law Harry Rankin.

Rankin shrugged. The Vanderhoof gymnasium was not the most primitive setting in which he had practiced his trade over the years.

Murray Miller slumped into his seat. "Never mind," he said to no one in particular. "We have just a few more hours of this—I heard we have the use of the Legion tomorrow."

"Thank God!" said one of the court officials sitting at the end of the table.

NICHOLAS FRIEMARK, eighteen years old and one of the non-Native witnesses, took the stand. Macarthur followed the procedure which he had used earlier with other witnesses at the scene of the accident—he read the statement which young Friemark had given to Constable Taylor and then asked for confirmation of the facts in that statement.

Like previous witnesses, Nicholas' statement related that he and his friends were at the bottom of Kenney Dam hill after the street dance, that a group of Natives went by and that a name-calling feud developed between the two groups. "They walked up past 6th Street and we stopped at 6th Street and Kenney Dam Road. . . . I heard a vehicle turn on to Kenney Dam Road. . . . As it started to approach us, we all moved off the road. I looked up the hill and there was no one on the road . . . then I turned to talk to Shorty Inkster and then I heard the vehicle's brakes lock up, squealing tires and a thump." He thought, he said, that the Redekop vehicle was going about forty-five miles an hour. "We all had been drinking," said his statement, "that is, the people in our group."

Under cross-examination, Nicholas said that he didn't actually see Coreen cross the road. Moreover, he admitted that when he said the speed of the Redekop vehicle was forty-five miles per hour, this estimate was strictly a guess.

THROUGHOUT THE AFTERNOON hearing, there had been several references to an Indian girl who was with "the white guys." This girl turned out to be Michelle Stewart, age fifteen, who now moved into the witness stand.

In Michelle's statement, after describing the name-calling which went on between the two groups there on Kenney Dam hill, she said that she was afraid that a more physical confrontation might develop. She related how she went further up the hill and "told Sharon Raphael that I wasn't with those [white] guys if they started fighting." Having established her role in case of a fracas, she returned to Shorty Inkster, Henry Reddecopp and the rest. In her statement Constable Taylor asked, "Did you hear anyone say, 'Let's play chicken'?" "No," answered Michelle.

Her statement went on: "Question: What took place as the car came up the road? Answer: Well, she [Coreen] was standing there like she was going to go to the other side where the girls were, then she just stood there and the car was just a few feet

115

from her and she just ran out in front and the car hit her." Coreen had been standing on the very edge of the pavement on the right hand side. "It looked like she just ran out in front of the car."

"Oh God," moaned Sophie quietly. Every time she heard the words, "She ran in front of the car," it was as if Coreen's death was happening all over again.

Under cross-examination Michelle admitted that from where she was standing, "It looked like she ran out in front of the car, but I'm not saying that for sure because I don't see very well." She said she wore glasses and that she was wearing them on the night of the accident. She thought the Redekop vehicle was travelling pretty fast, but she could not estimate the speed. When Rankin questioned her about the amount she drank the night of the street dance, he found it necessary to reassure her—he did not want, he said, to embarrass her or get her into trouble. The young girl responded that she had had five or six beers during the street dance.

Sid Simons questioned the witness about the "chicken" business.

"I want you to think back on it and think whether anybody that was there on the roadway that night was playing chicken."

"I can't remember anybody playing chicken at all," answered Michelle.

"You know what that means, don't you?"

"Yeah, I do."

"What do you understand it to mean?"

"I'm not sure."

"Well, what's your best understanding of it?"

Michelle's answers were barely audible. "I don't know."

"You've heard the expression, have you?"

"Yes, I have."

"I mean before today?"

"Not really."

"Did you hear anybody mention that expression that morning?"

"No, I didn't."

IF THE LAWYERS, THE CORONER, or the jurors had experienced a strain in trying to hear witnesses earlier, their problem was intensified when Margie (Marjorie) Thomas, Coreen's young sister, took the stand. Margie, a petite girl in jeans and a white nylon jacket who appeared younger than her fourteen years, looked terrified. More than one person thought that she would collapse even before questioning had begun. A worried Sophie Thomas leaned forward in her seat as if a little extra nearness might help to support Margie.

Cliff Macarthur explained to the witness that he would read the statement she had made to Constable Taylor and that she would then be asked to confirm the truth of the statements she had made. As Macarthur read, it was obvious that the constable had experienced difficulty in taking Margie's evidence; she had responded only to questions in her session with him.

In part her statement was as follows:

"Question: What did you do after the street dance?

"Answer: Went to the Vanderhoof Hotel to see if Coreen could go back to her room. That woman wouldn't let her go up because she had lost the key.

"Question: Were you drinking?

"Answer: No.

"Question: Was or had Coreen been drinking?

"Answer: Yes, in her room.

"Question: Was she drinking at the street dance?

"Answer: Shook head in negative."

The constable then turned to the matter of a yellow car which had driven up Kenney Dam hill just before the accident. Was Margie or anyone with her playing chicken with this car? Margie answered in the negative.

"What happened after this yellow car went by?" asked the constable.

"We started walking again."

"With all this walking, you should be in Stoney Creek by now," said the constable, according to the words read by Macarthur.

Towards the end of the statement, the constable had asked Margie, "Did she [Coreen] walk out in the path of the car?" Margie had nodded her head. The constable then asked, "Who said, 'Let's play chicken'?"

Margie had answered, "Coreen said it, I think."

As he had with the other witnesses, Cliff Macarthur asked Margie, "Is that the statement you gave to Constable Taylor?"

"Yes," said Margie.

"And is it true?"

"Some of it is," replied Margie. "That chicken is a mistake."

Cliff Macarthur was obviously taken aback. "Pardon me?"

Margie's voice was barely audible. "He made me say [it]. That chicken is not true. . . . He made me say it because I was last when he ask[ed] me questions."

There was a long pause. Despite the dreadful acoustics, a dropped pin could have been heard—the silence was deafening.

Finally Macarthur asked, "How did he make you say it? Margie, what did he do to make you say it?"

"Nothing," whispered Margie. "Just told me if I don't say it he say[s] I'm lying."

"You say the policeman told you to say it?"

Margie was crying. "Forced me to say it. . . . He said those other guys with you, they played chicken so I had to say it."

"Was Coreen playing chicken?" asked Macarthur.

"No," whispered Margie.

When Macarthur motioned to Simons and Rankin to commence cross-examination, the coroner interjected. "Well, I'm just wondering if we want to get into this now. I've made arrangements for supper with the jury at 5:30."

"It's a nice time to break," said Harry Rankin.

"And this might be a good time to break and of course we'll have to recall . . . we're talking about Constable Taylor, aren't we, in this conversation?"

"Yes, Your Honour," replied Cliff Macarthur.

As the gymnasium emptied, and as Harry Rankin and Murray Miller moved towards Sophie Thomas, Margie could be seen crying quietly on her father's shoulder.

15

EVERY REPORTER AND BROADCASTER was at the press table when the hearing resumed at seven o'clock in the evening. One could envision the blazing headlines in the next day's newspapers—WITNESS ACCUSES CONSTABLE OF FORCING HER TO LIE—followed in a day or two by other headlines—CONSTABLE DENIES MAKING GIRL LIE.

The coroner opened proceedings. "The logistics of keeping this going, Mr. Foreman and Jurors," he said, "has been difficult. I believe some of you have domestic duties, but you have agreed to come back at 9:30 tomorrow when we have made arrangements for the Legion to be available. . . . And I also want to thank the school board and the principal of the school for allowing me to take the blackboard with us tomorrow as well as the P.A. system."

The coroner went on to make a request on behalf of the jurors. Could the lawyers question the witnesses in language which the witnesses could understand? "Was that your question, Mr. Foreman?" asked the coroner.

"Yes," replied Ken Luggi. "We feel the witnesses should be questioned in simple English and not in lawyer's language. . . ."

"Lawyers have been speaking too long in lawyer's language," interjected Harry Rankin.

"I'm afraid we're all guilty of that as we go along," said the coroner. Turning to Cliff Macarthur he said, "You have another request, I believe, in connection with the TV matter."

120

"Yes, Your Honour," replied Macarthur. "It is with respect to television cameras. I understand they [the cameramen] wished to film the proceedings at the inquest. I myself have no objection to that. I am, however, concerned with television cameras being beamed on the witnesses as they are testifying. I would think that might be somewhat intimidating to them."

"I think it is, too," said the coroner. "I think the closer we can get to the natural way of doing things—nothing here is natural really, but we'll do our best. I think the media will understand that, and that is my ruling." He turned to the lawyers' table. "Mr. Rankin. . . . "

MARGIE THOMAS WAS BACK on the stand; more than once Harry Rankin asked, "Can you speak just a little bit louder? Nobody is going to bother you." At one point the coroner suggested turning up the volume on the microphone, then added ruefully, "But if it's turned up too far, it squeaks. . . . "

Softly, almost in whispers, Margie told of going to the police station and spending an hour and a half there giving her evidence to Constable Taylor. Did she understand, asked Rankin, the questions which the constable put to her? Repeatedly, Margie answered that she did not.

Rankin read from the statement. " 'Question: With all this walking, you should be in Stoney Creek now.' Did you know what he meant by that?"

"No."

"Then he said to you, 'Did she walk out in the path of the car?' . . . and you said, ' "Uh, yes" and then nodded the head in the affirmative.' Do you know what that means? . . . Do you remember doing that?"

"No."

"When you were asked, 'Did she walk out in the path of the

car?' . . . It means did Coreen walk out . . . as the car went up the road from here [pointing to the blackboard] in that direction?"

"No . . . she didn't walk out in the road."

Taking up Margie's statement again, Rankin read, " 'Question: Who said, "Let's play chicken"?' Do you remember him asking you that question?"

"Yes," Margie whispered.

"And you said, according to him, 'Coreen said it, I think.' Now, did Coreen say anything about playing chicken?"

"I didn't heard [hear] her say that . . . the policeman was mean to me . . . he made me cry."

"He made you cry," repeated Rankin. "I see. Were you scared of the police office?"

"Yes."

IT WAS NOW SID SIMONS' TURN to cross-examine Margie. "Hello, Margie," he said. "My name is Simons and I'm a lawyer here like Mr. Rankin, only he's bigger than me and he's got more grey hair. Okay? . . . If you don't understand any questions I'm asking you, you ask me to ask it again. Okay?"

In answer to Simons' questions, Margie affirmed that she had not read over her statement until that day, when she was waiting to testify.

"Now, after the five typewritten pages we have a drawing on there. . . . Do you know what it's a picture of?"

Margie's answer was almost inaudible and had to be repeated. "The hill where Coreen got hit."

With much probing and repetition of questions, Margie said that on the day when Constable Taylor took her evidence, she pointed to the spots on the drawing where she and her group had been standing on Kenney Dam Road where Coreen was struck by the vehicle and the constable had made marks—she had not made any marks herself on the drawing of the accident scene.

Simons turned to the matter of speed.

"Who told you that the car was coming up the hill going seventy miles an hour?" he asked.

"Myself."

"Pardon?"

"Myself."

"I didn't hear you, dear. What did you say?"

Margie was weeping as if she would never stop. "Myself."

"Yourself. Well, how could you tell?"

"Going fast."

"Well, going twenty miles an hour would be fast for some of us, wouldn't it?"

"Yes."

Simons turned to Margie's interview with Constable Taylor. "Now when you were talking to the policeman, you were talking to Constable Taylor, right? . . . A nice tall man, right? . . . Was he nice to you, Margie, or did he talk bad to you?"

"Talked bad."

"He talked bad. The whole time he was with you did he talk bad? . . . And did he ask you at the end of it if everything that you told him and that he wrote down was true?"

"No."

"He didn't ask you that?"

"No."

As the questioning went on, Margie's aunt and her parents looked increasingly worried. Her father wanted to interfere; he wondered if there was something he could do to help her. In the end he sat quietly, his body tense, his only gesture a movement to cover his eyes with a hand. If he had been asked why he didn't take his daughter from the witness stand and out of the room, he would have said, if he could have found the words, that he was an Indian who had no confidence that anything he could do would change this drama. Some of the Natives looked at Murray Miller, the family lawyer, as if to demand that he, at least, should do something. He could only shrug in reply. Legal etiquette allowed him no dramatic gesture, no Hollywood-style intervention.

SUDDENLY SID SIMONS BEGAN questioning Margie about another statement which she had signed. It appeared that an insurance adjuster from the Insurance Corporation of British Columbia had called on the Thomas home on Stoney Creek Reserve on July 29 and, as part of his investigation, a statement had been taken from Margie. Simons, Rankin, and the coroner discussed the validity of the adjuster's statement, or even the relevancy of it—occasionally a voice from the audience added to the confusion by identifying himself as the adjuster under discussion. When it was learned that the adjuster was under subpoena to appear, the coroner had another concern. "If he's going to be called in court, I don't think he should be in here listening."

Macarthur hastened to assure the coroner that the adjuster would not be called to give evidence.

"That's fair enough," said the coroner. "Don't mind us too much, Margie. We'll let you finish testifying in a moment here."

But within a very few minutes and a very few more questions in cross-examination, it became evident that Margie could not go on. She was crying uncontrollably and looked as if she might faint.

"Are you okay, Margie?" Simons asked. "Would you like a drink of water?"

The coroner intervened. "Well, I was afraid this would develop. I'll stand adjourned for a few minutes if she wants to compose herself, and we can come back. Otherwise—are you going to be all right, Margie?" The coroner looked rather helplessly from the weeping girl in the witness stand to the audience, then back again. "I think she can stand down and you can question her tomorrow. Are any of her next-of-kin here looking after Margie? After all, she's a juvenile. Are there any family here?" he asked more loudly.

Murray Miller stood up. "Her parents are here, Your Honour, and they have advised me that she is supposed to go back to school tomorrow. It's fairly important to her. I believe her father is right here."

The coroner looked annoyed. "Well, I think her own health and this procedure is far more important than going back to school. Let's get some humanity into this!"

As Margie was helped from the stand, a juror, a Native woman, spoke up. "Your Honour, may I ask a question?"

"Yes, please," said the coroner.

"Would it be possible tomorrow morning when Margie comes back to be accompanied by Mary John? . . . Mary John was the adult who took her to the police station, and she would I'm quite sure be able to tell Margie what is happening and be able to tell us what Margie was saying." Mary John nodded her agreement.

The coroner looked relieved. "I think so. I have no objection to that at all. Mr. Macarthur, would you call your next witness, please?"

THAT NEXT WITNESS was another young Native girl, Donna Patrick, sixteen years old, pale with long straight hair and a frightened demeanor which soon dissolved into tears. Once again the effort to hear her was unimaginably difficult for the court reporter, the jurors, the coroner.

Her statement, as read to her by Cliff Macarthur, told of how she and Lawrence Johnny took a short-cut to join Coreen and her friends on Kenney Dam hill. According to this statement, the name-calling mentioned in other statements began. At one point the feud heated up and, as insults were hurled back and forth, Sharon Raphael gave Donna a shoe to use as a weapon of defence, and Coreen picked up a big rock. Although the fight did not materialize, the name-calling apparently continued.

Donna's statement went on to describe the passing of a yellow car—"Coreen tried to hitchhike it"—and continued: "Then this other car turned the corner as the yellow car had gone up the road. Then that car started coming up. It was speeding real fast. I could hear Coreen say, 'Let's play chicken,' then that car started coming towards us and then all of us people moved to the sides. I guess then Coreen turned around to get off the road, and then that car hit her. That car was going fast too. I don't know how fast. . . . She was trying to hurry across, but she was too slow because she was carrying . . . I guess she thought she was going to make it across. . . . [This playing chicken] when she, like, you just stand on the road, you see whether that car will hit you or stop or go off the road, unless you want to run off the road."

When he finished reading the statement, Macarthur asked Donna, "Did you give that statement to Constable Taylor?"

"There's one part that's wrong," she whispered. "Playing chicken."

Macarthur read her part of the statement: " 'I could hear Coreen say, "Let's play chicken." ' Is that true? Is that true?"

"No."

"Pardon?"

"No."

"Did you say that to Constable Taylor?"

"He forced me to say it."

"Pardon?"

"He forced me to say it. . . . He said he could easily send me away."

"Can you tell me what his words were?"

"If you don't tell me, he [I] could easily send me [you] away somewhere."

BARBARA KOBIERSKI FROM the Native Programs Section of the Legal Services Commission, employed as manager of the Native Courtworkers and also a member of the Indian Home-makers, gave up trying to hear Donna Patrick's soft voice and made some notes for the report that she would have to present when the inquest was over.

She was aware of the fear and tension which had been building between the Native and white communities since the inquest had begun, and she wrote, as if to remind herself of this atmosphere: "On Saturday night we were driving home after the inquest and saw two Indian girls walking up that same road on their way home to Stoney Creek. We stopped and were going to offer them a ride home. When we started to slow down, they ran and hid in a nearby yard and never did come out."

HARRY RANKIN WAS INTO his cross-examination for only a few moments when it was discovered that there was a note on the back of the statement, apparently written by Constable Taylor.

"It seems to have some significance," said Rankin.

"Yes, I would agree," said Macarthur. "It says, the best I can read it, 'Yellow car comes up—the road first.' And then, 'Donna, playing chicken. Me . . . ,' presumably Constable Taylor, ' "I want you to tell me the truth, Donna, not a story someone else told you, but the truth." Donna says . . . "The first story I told you was the truth, the one on the night of the accident," and then me,' presumably Constable Taylor, ' "The night of the accident you told me she was playing chicken with that car. Now, Donna, you're telling me a different story, that she was standing in the centre of the road and was walking to the left side. You're not telling the truth to me, you are lying to me, Donna." ' And there appears to be a signature of Constable Taylor, RCMP, dated the 5th of July, 1976, 7:29 p.m."

Rankin now made an effort to learn from Donna when the note on the back of the statement was written by the officer.

"After he wrote the statement," she said.

"After you made the statement?"

"After we had finished making the statement."

"All right, after you finished writing the statement, you said something to him about the chicken question not being true, is that right? Is that what you're saying?"

"Yes, sir."

Rankin turned to the coroner. "See," he said, "the language is most peculiar, Your Honour. I think that to some extent it says, 'The night of the accident you told me she was playing chicken with you that time. Now, Donna, you're telling me a different story, that she was standing in the centre of the road and was walking over to the side. You are not telling me the truth. You are lying to me, Donna.'"

Cliff Macarthur nodded. "I might say, I intend to call Constable Taylor."

"He's going to have to be recalled," said the coroner. "There's no question about that."

"I think I may be wasting my time with this girl," Rankin said.

The coroner continued to look at the handwritten note which had been passed to him. "This is almost like a memo to oneself," he mused. He shook his head. "I can't figure this out."

SID SIMONS' CROSS-EXAMINATION was brief, and Murray Miller said that he had no questions to ask of Donna. Obviously, none of the lawyers were prepared to go further in cross-examination until Constable Taylor could be questioned again.

The coroner seemed relieved. "I think frankly, Mr. Foreman and Jurors," he said, "and I think, Counsel, the strain of us trying to hear things is very tiring and I'd like to call it a day and come back at 9:30 tomorrow at the Legion."

Rankin asked if the next day would be a short one.

"A short day, well, I don't know," said the coroner. He turned to Macarthur. "Have you got many more witnesses lined up? . . . I don't want to do an inquest by attrition. I've got to consider my foreman and jurors."

When Macarthur replied that he had twelve more witnesses to call, the coroner could only say, "We will do our best tomorrow, hopefully."

ONE EVENING CLIVE COCKING, reporter for the *Vancouver Sun*, found Sid Simons angrily pacing barefoot up and down the floor of his motel room. Simons' wife Beverley, wrote Cocking, "sat on a bed interjecting bitter comments between bites of crackers and cheese. They were seething with anger at the 'persecution' of the Redekops in the press and through the trial-like atmosphere of the inquest. But they were particularly incensed with Harry Rankin's conduct.

" 'What it is, is a concerted effort to destroy this [Redekop] family,' fumed Sid, who ironically began his career in Rankin's firm. 'Harry seems to me to be completely indifferent to the fate of this family,' snapped Beverley. 'He's sacrificing individuals to a cause.' "

Earlier, Simons, talking to a CBC reporter, had expressed his anger, not at Harry Rankin, but at the biased reporting of the press. He had gone on to question the validity of the inquest itself. "The inquest," he said, "is fluctuating between a trial and a platform for social issues. It has been both and it was intended to be neither. It has been enlarged out of proportion and has become a public spectacle. They used to have them in London, public 'angings—I did in fact see a lady sitting knitting one of the days."

His wife felt even more strongly about the publicity; she pointed out bitterly that her husband's client was being made the scapegoat for age-old grievances. "I am glad Sid came up here," she said, "and I think Rick has had a far fairer hearing than he would have if we hadn't come up. And I would like to say why we did come—when I read the publicity that had already come up about this family—when Sid came home and presented it to me and said, 'Shall I go? I'll only go if you come with me,' I told our kids, 'I'm going,' because I was extremely upset, and I'm going to get upset again—I believe in principles and social issues, but never at the cost of sacrificing an individual, and when I see people who are speaking as though it's in the name of compassion and social concern, forgetting they are dealing with human beings—thank God, Sid can stand up to it and speak with less emotion. . . . "

By the time Mrs. Simons had uttered her last word, she was weeping freely.

16

THE BASEMENT OF THE LEGION, a long narrow room, seemed to many of the spectators to be a garish setting in which to probe the death of a young Native girl. Paper baubles hung from the ceiling, red, green, blue, orange, yellow. They stirred gently with the slightest movement in the hall, sometimes creating a rainbow of colour on the drab plaster. And there was the piano and there was the naked empty bar, mute evidence of jollier times in this setting.

All day people came and went. An enterprising reporter counted sixty "early birds" as he called the observers, but someone else, an hour later, counted one hundred men and women and young people—a few minutes after ten, a troop of high school students had moved silently into the room, their teacher herding them to seats with all the skill of a well-trained sheep dog.

Just before the inquest was resumed on this Monday morning, reporters for national papers and for the CBC-TV program *Man Alive* were at the press table, scribbling lead sentences which in varying descriptive phrases reported that the town of Vanderhoof was in shock after witnesses from the day before had accused the RCMP of questionable practices. To relieve the tedium, one reporter started a pool, the object of which was to guess when the inquest would end.

PROCEEDINGS OPENED WITH Cliff Macarthur announcing that Sid Simons did not wish Margie Thomas to be recalled, although arrangements had been made for her to continue in the witness stand, accompanied by elder Mary John.

"There is nothing to be gained," Simons said. "We are prepared to forego any additional cross-examination and have the crown proceed."

"I would like to recall Constable Taylor," said Macarthur.

Constable Taylor looked grim as he entered the witness stand. In response to questions put to him by Macarthur, he described the circumstances under which he took a statement from Margie Thomas. "I took her into the Highway Patrol office where I interviewed her. I started to talk to Margie Thomas. Asked her name. And before any conversation took place, she began to cry. I allowed Margie Thomas to cry. After she was settled down, I began to talk to her, found out her name, name of her mother, where she went to school, and then told her I wished to know what occurred the night her sister was killed."

"Yes," said Macarthur.

"And she broke down crying and I allowed her to cry and after she stopped, I continued and she related the story or the circumstances that evolved around the accident scene."

Taylor denied that he had threatened Margie in any way. Macarthur pointed out that Margie had stated the previous day that Constable Taylor had told her other witnesses had mentioned playing chicken and that she was expected to say this to the constable as well.

"That is not true," said the constable. "I prompted [asked] the question if Coreen had said, 'Let's play chicken.' And this question was prompted by my hearing from other witnesses that this was, in fact, so. I in no way forced or intimidated Margie Thomas to tell me anything."

When, asked Macarthur, did Constable Taylor first hear a suggestion that somebody was playing chicken?

"About thirty seconds after I arrived at the accident scene.

JUDGEMENT AT STONEY CREEK

. . . As I previously stated, I attended at the body of Coreen Thomas and checked for a pulse. I had some of the others remove Margie Thomas from her sister because she was crying over the body. I then spoke to Donna Patrick who was there also, who was quite calm and collected and Donna Patrick stated to me at that time, at the accident scene, that she [Coreen] was playing chicken. And she ran out on the road."

The constable then described the circumstances under which he took a statement from Donna Patrick. He stated that, as in Margie's case, he asked her a number of questions: her name, where she lived, etc. "During this initial conversation, not the written statement. . . . "

"As a preliminary to the written statement, is it?" asked Macarthur.

"That is correct. . . . She indicated to me different things that I did not know, the first being that there was also a yellow car had come up the hill. And this I wrote down on a piece of paper and she continued on with her conversation and she stated to me during this initial interview, that Coreen had been standing on the side of the road, rather than going out or playing chicken or running out to the road in front of this vehicle. At that moment I was listening to her and I did not recall that is what she had said the previous night and I made the comment to her that she was lying to me, because on the night when I spoke to her at the accident scene, she told me that she [Coreen] was playing chicken and ran out on the road. And I looked at my notes and I told her precisely that. I told her that I wanted her to tell me the truth. I did not want some prefabricated story or some story somebody told her to tell me."

In answer to a question from Cliff Macarthur, Constable Taylor said that during the preliminary interview he had said to Donna, "You are not telling the truth to me. You are lying to me, Donna."

Why, wondered Macarthur, had the constable said that to Donna?

"Because I didn't feel she was telling me the truth."

Just before Macarthur turned the constable over for cross-examination he asked, "What was your purpose in writing any of this down on the back of the sketch, if you will? What is the reason for recording bits and pieces of the preliminary conversation?"

The constable answered that in the preliminary conversation with Donna Patrick, she mentioned things such as the yellow car which he had not heard of before—he wanted to clarify certain things further or else to have points down for his own reference, not as part of a written statement.

"Did she [Donna] appear to want to speak to you freely?"

"Yes, she did to me. She was quite calm. She was quite vocal about it. I was having a hard time keeping up with what she had to say. I can only write a few words a minute."

"Did you threaten her or anything of that nature?"

"No, I did not."

"Did you ever say anything to her like, 'If you don't tell me the truth or don't tell me what I want to hear or mention this chicken business, I am going to send you away,' or anything like this?"

"No, I did not."

HARRY RANKIN'S OPENING questions concerned the length and kind of statement the constable had taken from Margie Thomas. Margie's statement, asserted Rankin, was longer than any other statement taken by the constable—double, for example, the statement taken from Richard Redekop.

Constable Taylor defended himself. "Obviously, if I was able to take a four-page statement from her, she wasn't crying all the time!"

"That is right," snapped Rankin. "You didn't take a statement from her at all. You never asked her for a statement like you did all the others or the majority of witnesses. You cross-examined or examined in chief, whatever you want. . . ."

"I don't believe so," said Taylor. He said that he had had to ask questions because Margie did not elaborate on any of her answers, either through fear or upset over her sister's death. "So to make it easier for her, I asked questions rather than letting her just sit there without saying anything. I wanted to know what hapened, so I asked her questions to find out what happened."

Rankin was not so easily satisfied. He went down the list—Richard Redekop, Henry Reddecopp, Mark Cormack, Faye Haugen—all of them first gave a statement and then answered questions. Not Margie Thomas, asserted Rankin. Why? Constable Taylor insisted that each case was different.

"Do you know who was driving the yellow car that came up the road?"

"No."

"Do you know yet?"

"No, I do not."

"Why not?"

Constable Taylor was getting riled. "Because I am not God!" he said angrily.

Rankin wondered about the yellow car, he said, "because you are saying a chicken game was played with that car as well?"

"That is correct," answered Taylor.

"And that would give some substance to that which came out of thin air, the chicken game was something you raised with Donna and the other girl?"

"I didn't raise the subject," the constable answered emphatically. "Donna Patrick raised that at the time of the accident when I arrived."

"You never told us that when you were in the witness box, did you?"

The constable was getting riled again. "I wasn't asked to tell you, so why should I tell you?"

"Witness," thundered Rankin, "you are asked to tell and assist this inquest in every possible way! You are raising the question of the discussion you had with Donna for the first time this morning on the chicken game!"

Macarthur intervened. "My recollection of the evidence, is this Constable, when he initially testified in chief, did say that someone had mentioned playing chicken."

Rankin denied this. It was, he insisted, never mentioned until this, the third day of the inquest. "Let me put it to you again, that you did not at any time on the first day of this inquest or any time during the inquest say that at the accident scene Donna Patrick said there was a game of chicken being played on that road!"

"I may have to agree with you because I do not. . . . "

"I don't want you to agree with me!" snapped Rankin. "I want you to say yes or no."

"I will not say yes or no," replied the constable, "because I don't know whether I did say yes or not!"

Once again Cliff Macarthur intervened. "Your Honour, in fairness to the witness, when he gave evidence initially, he was not asked to relate conversation from anybody . . . and he was asked at that time to respond to questions and to respond to questions only."

Harry Rankin looked at Macarthur, at the coroner, and then shrugged his shoulders. He changed the subject.

HE TURNED TO THE HANDWRITTEN note which seemed to appear almost by accident when Rankin had been cross-examining Donna the day before. Why, he wanted to know, was it not part of Donna Patrick's written statement which she read over and signed, and which would have been available to him during cross-examination of her and of Constable Taylor as well.

"This occurred prior to my taking this verbal written statement," said the constable.

"Why didn't you include it in your typewritten statement?"

The constable said that there are always preliminary remarks before a statement is taken down, and that this handwritten note fell into that category. "I don't want to just walk into an interview with a witness or an accused and start writing things down."

The lawyer was tenacious. "On your written words, your memo to yourself, as you call it, 'Me, I want you to tell me the truth, Donna, not a story that somebody else tells you to tell me.' Why wasn't that put in the statement as part of the information that we require at a hearing?"

The constable repeated, "That was not part of the verbal written statement."

The questions and answers followed thick and fast. Finally Rankin suggested that Taylor had left out his accusations that Donna was lying from the written statement "so the statement looks just the way you want it, nicely tailored."

The constable was stung into defending himself. "I never intimidated Donna Patrick and when I took the statement from her, I was quite calm and I was collected and I was not shouting at her or yelling at her as you are trying to implicate [insinuate] and I was very much more reserved in the way I spoke to Margie. In fact, I thought I was very soft-spoken with Margie!"

RANKIN TURNED TO THE CONSTABLE'S interview with Margie. he asked the constable to look at the statement of that interview. "You say you were being very mild with this girl. Playing it as cool as possible. Go to Page 3 below the middle of the page. 'With all this walking, you should be in Stoney Creek by now.' . . . Is that being mild?"

"I would almost say that would be a little more on the humourous side," replied Constable Taylor.

"How do you think she would appreciate this touch of humour?"

"She laughed."

"Do you remember that?"

"Uh-huh."

"Didn't put it down in the statement at all?"

"No. I can't put in every nod."

"You put in nods, didn't you? 'Nods her head in the affirmative.' "

Once more the constable was getting snappish. "I can use a tape recorder, if you want—you can't use those."

"Why not?"

"I didn't have one. They are not admissable."

Rankin was equally snappish. "They are admissable and you can use them. So you will know in the future."

"Okay."

Rankin went on, "I am suggesting to you that this is what I would call a laundered statement, all cleaned up and neat and in package and what you didn't want to put down, you put into notes in your book or remembered today. In other words, this is a statement that you consider to be . . . "

"A statement of Margie Thomas, yes," interrupted the constable.

"But not a complete statement. There were other words used that are not here . . . and in the case of Donna Patrick, that there are other words that are not here?"

"Prior to, yes."

"So that finally becomes what you consider the best," persisted Rankin, "you consider to be the best possible statement from your police investigation point of view?"

"Yes. And that is the statement as I took it."

"I am suggesting to you the best statement possible is everything they say."

Constable Taylor agreed but added, "You can have the statement that I gave to you and you can take the witness or the accused or whomever that are giving their testimony at the inquest . . . and you can decipher the truth from that."

Rankin was determined to have the last word. "But you can only decide that when you have all the material that the witness spoke to you brought forward by the officer that is investigating."

THERE FOLLOWED AN INSPECTION of the constable's notebook and the references to the chicken game in it.

"Did anybody else mention the chicken game at all? Did Margie mention it at the scene?" asked Rankin.

Constable Taylor replied that the phrase "playing chicken" was mentioned only by Donna Patrick. He added that she was not the only one who said that Coreen had run out on the road.

"You understand that a person can run out on a road through panic, inadvertence, or anything else? The chicken game, it is a deliberate playing a game with a car. You know that?"

"Yes."

Hypothetical cases were thrown back and forth between the constable and the lawyer in an effort to establish what was most germane to this case—the chicken game, or the act of running out on to the road. But ever and again, Rankin returned to what he regarded as a self-serving action on the part of the constable—during his day in the witness stand, the constable had not mentioned Donna speaking of the chicken game the night of the accident, and he had made no mention on that first day of testimony that Donna had changed her story and that he had accused her of lying.

"That is scribbling prior to a written statement!" snapped the constable. "Have you written down everything I have said? No. And that is what this is, just words of an interview!"

"But I can assure you of this," rumbled Rankin, "I have written down everything important that you said and every other witness at this inquest and I can tell you this, you didn't say anything about this the first day you were in the stand!"

Once again Macarthur intervened. "I think it is unfair to continue to ask the constable why he didn't say something when he wasn't asked."

Sid Simons interjected that there might have been some discussion of these matters between the lawyers on the evening before the inquest began.

Rankin cut in: "There wasn't any discussion with me." He turned on Simons. "I wish you wouldn't give evidence unless you want to go in the witness box!"

The coroner intervened. "We have gone a long way and we have a long way to go."

"I hope it is time for a coffee break," said Simons.

It was.

AFTER MURRAY MILLER HAD ASKED the constable a few questions concerning his accident report, the jurors requested additional information.

"Constable, it is normal for a police officer to question a juvenile without the presence of an adult?" asked the foreman.

The constable answered that if a juvenile is charged an adult must be present but, "if I am going to interview a juvenile who is a witness, there is no law that says I have to have a parent or guardian present."

Another member of the jury wondered if Coreen was covered with a blanket when Constable Taylor arrived at the scene, and the coroner asked about the emergency equipment that RCMP vehicles carry. The coroner also wanted to know what information the Vanderhoof coroner Eric Turner had been given by

Constable Taylor which made Turner originally decide on an inquiry as opposed to an inquest.

Constable Taylor replied that he had phoned a verbal report to Turner the morning of the accident.

"I did not have any written statements then."

"You did have in your notebook a little statement about the chicken. . . . Did you tell Coroner Turner about that?"

"I believe I told him that she ran out in front of the car. I do not recollect telling him that she was playing chicken." Constable Taylor added that subsequently he forwarded the written statements along with his police report to Turner.

"So far as you are aware, Coroner Turner would have no more information than that which you gave him?"

"That is correct."

The coroner wondered if Turner had had access to the constable's handwritten note which began with "yellow car."

"I cannot state whether he had that or not."

The coroner was not quite satisfied. Wouldn't Turner be very dependent on the information which the constable gave him from the scene?

The constable mentioned other police reports as well as his own; perhaps also Turner had interviewed witnesses himself without informing the constable.

Constable Taylor, looking weary and drained, left the witness stand.

17

THE PARTICIPANTS IN THE Vanderhoof hearing—lawyers, reporters, witnesses—by now were aware that the inquest had become a cause célèbre across Canada. Television screens beamed pictures of the inquest into living rooms from Labrador in the east to Alert Bay in the west. The hill where Coreen was killed, the main street in Vanderhoof on a Sunday afternoon, the crowds hurrying by foot and car and pickup truck away from the high school at the end of a day's hearings—these images became familiar sights to people from one end of Canada to the other.

What had began as a brief article in a local newspaper some months before the death of an Indian girl had escalated into an exposé of the reality of aboriginal life, not just in central British Columbia but throughout Canada.

For a time, if only briefly, there was a period of soul-searching. Once again many Canadian citizens faced the fact that inequalities still existed in this country called by its then-Prime Minister as the Just Society.

Questions were asked in "Letters to the Editor" columns and on open-line radio programs; the office of the Minister responsible for Indian Affairs in Ottawa was overwhelmed with irate calls; and the telephone lines into Vanderhoof were jammed with comments and appeals for information. Why, asked the questioning public, had an inquest into Coreen's death not occurred as a matter of course and without the need of pressure from her community? How could it happen in this country that a person was placed in a morgue without being declaired dead? Why would a constable of the famed Royal Canadian Mounted Police threaten frightened little Indian girls? With all the evidence of alcohol and excessive speed why was Richard Redekop not charged with something—anything? What was happening to the tax dollars which were to provide decent housing and services for Natives? Above all, why did Canada have, or appear to have, two justice systems, one for Natives and another for non-Natives?

Unlike their white compatriots, the aboriginal people were neither scandalized nor shocked at the evidence emerging from the Vanderhoof inquest. They were aware that the racism exposed during the course of the inquest was only the tip of the iceberg. They knew that there was scarcely an Indian in Canada who did not have a story to tell which would make the evidence at the Vanderhoof hearing sound like a bedtime story. One of these stories might have been told by the Micmac of the Membertou Reserve in Cape Breton concerning Donald Marshall, in 1976 a young man of nearly twenty-four who had already served five years in jail for a murder he did not commit. The Cree in The Pas, Manitoba—they could speak of Helen Betty Osborne, murdered in 1971. Five years later no one had been charged in her murder, although half the town of The Pas knew the four men whose names were linked to her death.

Who can doubt that the aboriginal people in Cape Breton and Manitoba and everywhere in Canada thought, as they listened to reports of the Vanderhoof inquest, that they had a few stories of their own that they could tell.

WHEN CONSTABLE TAYLOR left the witness stand, Cliff MacArthur made a proposal.

"Your Honour, I have discussed the next procedures with my friends and I think we are all in agreement that what we are going to do now is read the five statements of Kevin Inkster, George Patrick, Barry Quaw, Bruce Allan, and Vincent Sam. I think my friends undertook not to cross-examine various witnesses I understand to be out in the witness room. I would think if the jury wants any one of those witnesses, they could be made available, but at this time, in order to expedite matters, we intend simply to read the statements in."

The coroner nodded and Macarthur began with the statement of Kevin John Inkster, known as "Shorty" to his friends. The gist of his statement was that he was fifteen years old, that he thought the Redekop vehicle was going about forty miles an hour, and that he did not actually see Coreen being struck by the car because his back was turned. Kevin did not think that Richard Redekop sounded his horn as he drove up Kenney Dam hill.

The statement of George Barton Patrick, age twenty, was read into the evidence. "The [Redekop] car went around a little curve and Coreen, who was pregnant, was kind of slow moving off the road and the car hit her on the side. I didn't actually see her get hit by the car, but as I turned around, I saw her flying and the car stop." He said that he couldn't estimate the speed of the vehicle but it was "travelling pretty fast." He said that he had been drinking that night.

Next came the statement of Barry Joseph Quaw, age sixteen. He said that he and Coreen's brother Richard were up on an embankment on the east side of the road when they heard a car coming from town up the hill. "He was going really fast. I looked at the people who were standing on the road and most of them moved to the east side of the road. By the time I looked back, the car was very close to Coreen, and I heard it slam on its brakes. Then I heard a bang and turned around and said to Richard, 'Let's go down there. I think that's your sister.' " Barry thought the car was going faster than thirty miles per hour.

The statement of Bruce Morgan Allan followed. Bruce, age fifteen, lived in Fraser Lake, a community about forty miles west of Vanderhoof. He had been visiting his cousin, Vincent Sam, who lived near the accident scene. They left Vincent's home and were on Kenney Dam hill near 6th Street where they heard the two groups, white and Native, calling each other names. "We seen this car coming up the hill. It was coming sort of fast. I was looking towards the town and then I heard tires skidding and a 'thud.' " He thought the car was going about fifty-five or sixty miles an hour. He did not hear any of the Stoney Creek girls talk about "playing chicken."

Finally there was the statement of Vincent Allen Sam, age seventeen. "I was with Bruce Allan at the street dance. Then we went home to my place. After, Bruce and I . . . walked down the hill on Kenney Dam Road." As they were talking to the two groups, they saw a car coming up the hill. "We were already on the side of the road so we didn't have to move. Nick [Friemark] didn't bother to move, he was standing almost in the middle of the road. Then the car went around Nick. So I took a quick glance up the hill. Then I looked at Nick. Then I looked at the car. Then I heard the car start screeching or skidding or whatever it is. Then he just hit her." He saw Coreen on the side of the road, but he did not see her move to cross the road. Vincent thought the Redekop vehicle was going about sixty miles an hour.

"That concludes the statements that are going to be read," said Macarthur.

Now that the acoustics had improved, Sophie Thomas was able to hear every word which Cliff Macarthur read. Each time she heard the witnesses describe the impact when Coreen was struck, whatever phrases were used—"he just hit her," 'I saw her flying,' "I heard a thud"—she felt as if she was reliving Coreen's death over and over again. And as she listened to the witnesses estimate the speed of the Redekop vehicle, forty, fifty-five, sixty, or seventy miles per hour, anger heightened her grief. How come, she asked herself as she had a thousand times before, how come with those kinds of speed me and my people had to go through so much to have a hearing into Coreen's death?

THE REMAINDER OF THE MORNING and part of the afternoon were devoted to examining and cross-examining three more eyewitnesses at the accident scene: Sharon Raphael, age eighteen, Charlie Johnny, age twenty-six, and Cecil Raphael, in his twenties.

Efforts were made by the lawyers to pinpoint where each of the witnesses was when the Redekop vehicle began its ascent of Kenney Dam hill, to obtain their estimate of where Coreen was on the road before the accident, and to assess how much of the accident each witness had actually viewed.

Sharon Raphael's answers often contradicted each other and efforts to have her use a drawing or a photograph to place herself or Coreen at an actual spot on the road appeared to confuse her further. "Perhaps I could make a suggestion," said Rankin during Sid Simons' cross-examination. "The picture faces north. The drawing faces south. How anyone is going to get them squared around. . . . "

Simons denied that he was responsible for this difficulty.

"I'm not saying that," Rankin said. "Maybe you can explain it."

"I'm trying to get there," said Simons. "I am trying to 'unconfuse' her, not confuse her, if I can."

In other areas, Sharon seemed more certain. She thought the Redekop car was going about seventy or eighty miles per hour coming up the hill.

"Did you see Coreen get hit by the car?" asked Rankin.

"No. Just seen her going to the other side of the road. And

the car was coming at her."

"Did you see her get hit or dragged by the car?"

"No. Just seen her flying."

Sharon said that she had just one bottle of beer that evening. She said that she had been up in Coreen's hotel room, but whether she had the beer in the hotel room or later, at the street dance, she couldn't be certain. She said that so far as she knew, there was only one case of beer in the hotel room.

"Do you know how much beer Coreen had to drink?" asked Simons.

"No."

"No idea? You are shaking your head, Sharon. Can you tell us what you mean, yes or no?"

"No."

"Did you see her drinking at the dance?"

"Yes. Just one."

"Did you see her drinking beer in the hotel room?"

"Yes."

"Do you know how many you saw her drink there?"

"No."

Although the lunch hour intervened, Sid Simons resumed questioning Sharon afterwards. "Sharon," he asked, "when most of you crossed the road, Coreen went to the other side of the road when the car was coming, is that correct?"

"Yes."

BARBARA KOBIERSKI FROM THE Legal Services Commission cornered Cliff Macarthur during one of the breaks. She had watched many of the young Natives, ending with Sharon Raphael, undergoing examination by the lawyers. She had watched their confusion as they tried to respond to questions which they often did not understand.

"Can't you get the lawyers to speak in simpler terms?" she

asked Macarthur. "I hear them using words like 'presuppose' and 'recapitulate'—these words are not in the vocabulary of the Indian witnesses. They think in Carrier and then reply in English. It's a real ordeal for them."

Macarthur nodded. He often saw this same problem in communication in Prince George, where about three-quarters of his cases dealt with Native people. He knew that the whole court system was alien to them. He agreed with Barbara that the Indians were caught up in a justice system which they simply did not understand.

CHARLIE JOHNNY said he was walking down into the ditch just before the accident, and in doing so, he walked past Coreen. Moments later, when he had his back to her, she was hit. He said he had been drinking that night, but did not believe that he was drunk. Like other witnesses, he said that he heard squealing tires and a thump, then saw Coreen flying through the air.

"Did you form an impression as to the speed of the car?" asked Harry Rankin.

"It was going pretty fast. How far it skidded!"

"Are you able to estimate what you mean by 'pretty fast'?"

"About sixty anyways."

WHEN CECIL RAPHAEL APPEARED in the witness stand, a wave of anticipation was almost visible in the Native groups scattered at the back of the Legion Hall. Raphael had come in from the ranch where he worked to give his evidence. He was considered something of a wild man in the Indian community—the people who knew him felt he would be able to hold his own in the witness box.

However, this was not Raphael's first appearance at the inquest. During Day One of the hearing, he had been described by Constable Taylor as intoxicated at the accident scene. When James Morris, who lived within yards of the site, gave evidence at Day Two of the hearing, he described Cecil Raphael as appearing sober to him. In order to be certain of the identity of the man so described, Cecil Raphael was brought into the hearing room and Morris was able to affirm that this was the person he had talked to at the accident scene and who had seemed sober to him.

Raphael said that he had attended the street dance and was on his way to Stoney Creek, but stopped on Kenney Dam hill because he was waiting for a friend who was bringing him cigarettes. In addition, the Chief from Stoney Creek had promised to pick him up and give him a lift home. He said that he was anxious to leave his particular spot on the hill—he heard the argument going on between the two groups and wanted to get away from "this little argument," as he called it.

"I heard a car coming and generally, you know, you are not looking to see who is on the road when you are standing in a place like that. I spun around and I caught a glimpse of somebody there. And from there, I seen the car strike and she [Coreen] was picked up—she was hit towards the front as she was trying to make her way. What was happening, I think, the lights were blinding her. . . . She was trying her best to get out of the way. I could see that."

He thought, he said, that the Redekop car was travelling sixty-five or seventy miles per hour and that the headlights were on bright.

Sid Simons wanted to clarify the matter of Raphael's sobriety. "Where did you do your drinking?"

"I had three bottles of beer."

"The whole night?"

"The whole evening, yes."

"That wouldn't cause you to be under the influence of liquor in any way, I guess then?"

"Well, let's say that three bottles of beer would never make any man drunk!"

He said that he had his last bottle of beer about three hours before the accident.

Simons turned to the matter of estimating the speed at which the Redekop vehicle had been travelling just before Coreen was struck. "Where do you get the figure sixty-five or seventy miles per hour, Cecil?" he asked.

"Because I have driven around about six to seven hundred thousand miles since I have had my own driver's licence and I happen to know what speed really is."

Simons wondered about this ability to assess the speed of the vehicle after observing it covering only two or three blocks. "With your vast driving experience, I hope you can help us by telling us at seventy miles an hour, how many feet per second a vehicle would travel."

Rankin was on his feet. "If he [Simons] wants to qualify this man for a witness . . . "

"He qualified himself!" said Simons quickly.

"Hold tight, Mr. Simons," rumbled Rankin. " . . . At any time when Counsel gets up and makes an objection, the other Counsel sits down and keeps quiet!"

The coroner intervened. "I already accepted your objection, Mr. Rankin, ahead of time. He [Raphael] is not an expert and he is not expected to be. . . . "

Simons was not satisfied with this ruling. "Your Honour, what has thrown me about this, my friend qualified him as a witness by giving an estimate of the speed between sixty-five and seventy miles an hour. . . . "

Rankin was on his feet again. "Every witness that gave evidence here did the same thing. It's an estimate." He picked up a small book from the table. "This is a chart that will give you feet per second and you can get it out [of there]."

"ANY QUESTIONS, MR. FOREMAN?" asked the coroner.

Ken Luggi nodded. The varying descriptions of Raphael's sobriety at the time of the accident obviously worried the foreman. "Cecil," he asked, "did Constable Taylor have anything to say to you at the scene?"

"He asked me if I was there and I said, 'Yes, I was.'"

"Did he ask you any questions?"

"He asked me if I had seen her hit and I said, 'I seen her, yes, flying through the air.' That is about it."

The coroner, too, had questions of Cecil Raphael: on what street—Fourth? Fifth?—did he first see the headlights of the approaching car? Was it a dark night or was the moon shining? He also asked Raphael to indicate on Exhibit 2A where he was at the fatal moment, to which Raphael complied.

"Thank you very much, Cecil," said the coroner.

18

S PECTATORS BEGAN TO SEE a pattern in what one lawyer called the "game plan" of the inquest. Cliff Macarthur and his colleagues had established what might be characterized as the forensic aspects of Coreen's death—evidence from the police, the ambulance driver, the doctor who performed the autopsy, the experts on vehicle speed and blood alcohol levels. There followed the evidence of eyewitnesses at the accident scene. Now the net was spread a little wider—staff members in the Vanderhoof Hotel and its owner were next to take the witness stand.

The desk clerk of the Vanderhoof Hotel, Margart Pocock, was summoned.

Looking very young for the position she held in the hotel, Margaret stated that she was on duty on the night of the street dance. She said that she knew Coreen by sight, and did see her during the night in question. On two occasions on the night of July 2, she heard a commotion in the area where Coreen had earlier rented a room. On the first occasion, about 6:30 in the evening, she went to Coreen's room. She found four people there, whom she could describe only as "Coreen Thomas, one of her sisters, a mute girl, and Sharon somebody. . . . They were drinking. . . . It was noisy down there. They were more or less quite noisy. . . . I asked them to quiet down.

"Half an hour later," she continued, "they were making more noise and I again told them to quiet down, which they refused to do."

"What was Coreen's condition at this time as to sobriety?" asked Macarthur.

"You could call her more or less sober."

"Did you see Coreen or any of these girls again that evening?"

"It was after eleven o'clock. . . . Coreen and another girl were going to go up to the room. And one could go up but the other could not."

Why was this? wondered Macarthur.

"The room was paid for for two people and there was going to be three people when they went up after eleven o'clock." Three people in that room, said Margaret, was against a regulation of the hotel.

"They said they were just going to get something, and I okayed it. And they didn't come right down, so I sent up the manager."

"And what was Coreen's condition at this time, as you observed it, as to sobriety?"

"She was—she had a few drinks."

"Did you see Coreen again that evening?"

"No, I never."

SANDY INGRAM, MANAGER OF the Vanderhoof Hotel at the time in question, was called to the stand.

He stated that Coreen was known to him, and that sometime on the night of the street dance, between midnight and two o'clock in the morning, she came to him and asked that he switch part of the room to a younger sister.

"Did you go along with that?" asked Macarthur.

"Yes."

"What was her condition as to sobriety?"

"She was appearing normal. She wasn't intoxicated."

"Did either yourself or any employee of the hotel, to your knowledge, tell Coreen she couldn't stay in the room of the hotel that evening because she had lost her key or anything to that effect?"

"No."

Harry Rankin wanted to explore the matter of the hotel regulation. "Your rule is two people to a room?" he asked. Not necessarily, was Ingram's reply. In the room under discussion, there was only a double bed and it was this which determined that only two people should be in the room.

In response to further questions from Rankin, Ingram said that he had known Coreen since January, had seen her on a number of occasions, and had never seen her intoxicated.

"Your best opinion on that night [is that] she was not intoxicated?"

"No."

The coroner paused. "Who checked out of the room the next morning?" he asked.

"Mildred and one of her younger sisters. I don't know her name and I don't know if I would know her if I were to see her. Just a little girl, probably [age] ten or twelve."

"Any statement that says, in effect, the deceased was refused admission that night because she had lost her key is not true?" continued the coroner.

"Not any of my staff refused her entry," said Ingram emphatically.

JOHN FUITE, OWNER OF THE Vanderhoof Hotel (or as he said, "Well, I own half of it"), took the stand.

He said that he knew Coreen Thomas and that on the night of the street dance, he saw her a couple of times after she registered—"Once, between nine and ten in the evening, and one time after that was probably around one o'clock in the morning," he said.

"And what was her condition as to sobriety on the latter occasion?" asked Macarthur.

"Didn't appear drunk to me," said Fuite. "She asked me to come up and see what I could do with her sister who was quite drunk. And I went upstairs with her and her sister had passed out in the hallway at the top of the stairs. . . . I picked her sister up and carried her down the hall and put her in the room and laid her on the bed."

In answer to further questions, John Fuite said, "I don't know of any occasion that she was refused admission."

SID SIMONS WAS ON HIS FEET as soon as John Fuite left the witness stand.

"I have another person I would like to have called as a witness," he said to the coroner. "She was called away from a job to be here."

The coroner cautioned him: "I can only recall that my reporter must go at four o'clock. The jury wants to go home too."

"So do I," responded Simons fervently. "This person I have just been able to locate. I would like to call Marjorie Weaver as a witness."

Marjorie Weaver, a small dark woman, affirmed that she lived just beyond Stoney Creek and that she had been driving a 1966 dark green Pontiac vehicle up Kenney Dam hill just a few minutes before Coreen was killed in the early morning of July 3rd—her best estimate was that she was on the hill about three o'clock in the morning. Her husband was a passenger in the car with her.

"I observed a group of people standing on the beginning of the hill," she said, "maybe twenty or twenty-five. . . . I would say teenagers and in their twenties."

"How many were on the roadway?" asked Simons.

"Most of them," Mrs. Weaver replied.

She said that the young people on the roadway stayed pretty well where they were as she approached them, and that she took evasive action to avoid them by driving around them. She did not see anyone trying to hitch-hike a ride with her. She said one person "just stood and waved his hand." She thought it might have been Charlie Johnny. As a precaution she had locked the door beside her. "I always do [that] if I see a group of people standing along the road."

"Is it correct, Mrs. Weaver, that you have been reluctant to come here as a witness," asked Simons, "because you are concerned that you don't want to disturb the good relations you have with the community?"

Rankin was on his feet. "Your Honour . . . "

"I can anticipate, Mr. Rankin," interjected the coroner. "The community are my foreman and jurors. They will hear all the evidence and come to their own conclusions . . . if what she has said is the truth, I take it that is exactly what you want her to say."

Sid Simons sat down. "Thank you, Mrs. Weaver."

HARRY RANKIN STOOD UP to cross-examine.

He established with Mrs. Weaver that she had seen the group of young people on the hill when she was about two blocks away. She thought she was probably going about thirty miles per hour at that moment. She then decreased her speed, she said, because she saw so many people and "they were partially covering the road."

"And when you got to 6th Street . . . what speed would you be doing there?"

"Maybe about ten miles [per hour]."

"Any trouble getting through the group of people at all?"

"No."

Nobody trying to get in front of her car, questioned Rankin? Anybody making threatening gestures?

"No," answered the witness. She said that if there had been just one person on the road, she would probably have picked him or her up, but that when the number of people was large, she would not stop.

"And so your relationship remained good then and remains good now in terms of the Native people?"

"Yes."

The coroner wondered if Mrs. Weaver had seen that elusive yellow car.

No, she replied, she had not seen a car of that description during her drive home that night.

"Thank you very much," said the coroner.

19

AT 3:20 IN THE AFTERNOON of Monday, September 27, Faye Haugen, described by witnesses as Richard Redekop's wife, was called to give evidence.

This twenty-one-year-old girl, attractive, her long hair a dark blonde colour, was clearly upset throughout her time in the witness stand. More than once she appeared close to collapse as the lawyers forced her mind back to the early morning hours of July 3, there on Kenney Dam hill.

"Faye," said Sid Simons, "I am going to read you firstly the typewritten copy of a statement dated at 8:30 p.m., 6th July, 1976."

Simons then read the following: "We [Richard Redekop and Faye] were at the street dance and we picked up the baby at the baby-sitters. Then we started home and were coming up on the Kenney Dam Road, when we saw about thirty people on the road ahead of us. We slowed down and they all started moving on to either side of the road, and we just continued on. Then this Coreen girl, she just darted out in front of the car. We slammed on the brakes, but we hit her anyway. We couldn't swerve because we would hit people on either side of the road. We both got out of the car and everyone was yelling to get an ambulance but no one was doing anything, so we drove down to the Chevron station and called the police and the ambulance."

As her statement continued, she said that her daughter Michelle was on her lap and Richard was driving the car when the accident occurred, and that the car's headlights were on. She couldn't remember if the horn had been sounded. She thought the vehicle was going about thirty miles per hour. "We weren't even out of the [town] limits yet."

In her statement Faye had been asked, "Did you see Coreen get hit by the car?" and she had answered, "It happened so fast. I don't want to do any more of this. Can I come in another day?"

"Did you return the following day?" asked Simons.

"Yes," answered Faye.

Sid Simons then proceeded to read the statement given the next day, July 7, 1976. During the taking of that statement by Constable Taylor, Faye was asked to indicate on a diagram where various people had been standing at the time of the accident. "I don't really remember," Faye had replied. "They were just standing all over the road. . . . Well, it just happened so fast, she was there and we hit her. We slammed on the brakes."

The statement indicated that Constable Taylor had drawn the skid marks on a diagram and pointing to them, he had asked Faye, "Now, can you tell me where Coreen was standing and where she came from when she was hit?"

Faye had answered, "No, I can't. When I think of it, it makes me sick."

"It makes her a lot sicker," the constable had replied.

"I can't see that," Faye had answered. "She's dead. I can see it making her family sick."

When Sid Simons finished reading this second statement, Faye confirmed that it contained the truth.

PUTTING THE STATEMENTS ASIDE, Simons continued questioning Faye.

"Had either of you been drinking anything in the nature of liquor or alcohol during the early morning?"

"We weren't both into drinking . . . with Bonnie [Bonnie Redekop, Richard's sister] being in the hospital and all . . . she was in critical condition."

"Your daughter Michelle is about two years old?"

"She is two today."

"And how long have you been living with Rick [Richard Redekop]?"

"About a year now."

"And what is Rick's relationship with Michelle?"

"He loves her."

"And he is treating her as though he were her real father?"

"He loves her."

Simons turned to Faye's level of activity when she was pregnant. "Were you able to move quickly? Were you able to climb stairs and do that sort of thing?"

Faye replied, "Yes, I just went about my daily thing as I normally did before I was pregnant."

Faye was questioned about Redekop's style of driving at the time of the accident.

"He was driving his usual way," she replied. She herself, she added, had been driving for two years.

"That was Rick's usual car that he drove [that night]?"

"No, it wasn't. It was a rented car."

"Are you able to say how long he had it?"

"I can't really remember. About two weeks."

MRS. REDEKOP, RICHARD'S MOTHER, looked tense and worried as she listened to Faye Haugen's evidence. One was reminded of Bishop Remi De Roo's description of this woman and her husband as people bewildered by the glare of publicity in which they so suddenly found themselves.

The bishop knew of the loss of two of their children through motor vehicle accidents. When he had talked to Mr. and Mrs.

Redekop during one of the breaks in the inquest, he felt that they were suffering very deeply. Said the bishop, "They are personally hurt at the accusations some people allegedly hurl at them of being 'murderers.' They hope that the many vicious rumours that are going around will cease as a result of the inquest and that the truth will come out fully. They are also very sensitive to the suffering of the Thomas family. I was able to convey to them the message that I had not picked up any vengeful or threatening expressions from the Indian leaders I had spoken to, and expressed the hope that full reconciliation could be brought about. This seemed to be their wish also."

When the bishop introduced himself to Richard Redekop during the inquest, he said that Richard seemed taken aback, and promptly excused himself, saying he had an errand to run. The cleric talked instead to Faye Haugen. "She impressed me," he wrote later, "as a quiet sensitive young woman. She seemed to share the Redekops' positive hopes that good might come out of all this pain."

NOW THIS QUIET SENSITIVE young woman was on the witness stand. She looked terrified as Rankin rose to question her.

"What happened to your regular car?" he asked.

"Someone stole it in Vancouver and rolled it," replied Faye.

Harry Rankin now tried to find out how far the Redekop car was from the people on Kenney Dam hill before Faye could see forms on the road. "When would you know they were people?"

"About 4th Street, because there was a light there."

"You were going approximately thirty miles an hour from the time you left the highway onto Kenney Dam Road . . . is that what you are saying?"

"Around thirty. We had slowed down when we first noticed people on the roadway."

"Your speed never exceeded thirty?"

"I don't think so. I really can't say."

"Could you have been going forty?"

"Could have been."

"Forty-five?"

"I don't think so. No."

Rankin now tried to establish where, in relation to the accident scene, the Redekop vehicle slowed down. "You want to take a short break?" he asked as Faye Haugen showed signs of distress. "I'll be okay," she said.

Rankin drew her attention to the map behind her. "Would you turn just a little to the right . . . and indicate where you slowed down?"

"I can't," she cried. "I told you, I can't!"

Rankin's voice softened. "Just look and please don't be upset. I will be as slow as I can on it. It is something I have to deal with."

"I know," Faye said numbly.

He tried, with the use of photographs, to get her to think back to the scene of the accident. Putting a photograph before her, he asked, "Does that help you a little bit in visualizing the scene?"

"I don't want to visualize it," she responded.

"None of us do," replied Rankin, "but it has to be done. That is a fact of life. And in ten minutes, it is finished with as far as you are concerned. Just one of those things that each of us has to do here."

He read from Faye's statement. " 'The crowds they all scattered to let us through.' . . . The word 'scattered' has a connotation of quick movement, running. Is that what you meant by the word 'scattered'?"

No, replied Faye. What she had really meant was that they casually went from either side of the road.

"And you say they moved at a slow pace off the road?"

"Not a slow pace, just to let us go through."

Rankin showed her a photograph of the hill and pointed to the skid marks. "Would you agree that this is where the skidding started?"

Faye began to weep. "I cannot really say because I can't remember much about that night. . . . It just happened so fast. They let us go through, so we kept on going and the road was clear. One moment she wasn't there and the next she was. I remember seeing her face. . . ." Faye turned very white and her body began to sag.

Macarthur intervened. "Perhaps, Your Honour, this will be an appropriate place for an adjournment."

Mary John watched Faye move to the doorway of the Legion Hall and gulp fresh air. She thought that the girl would surely faint.

WHEN THE FIFTEEN MINUTE recess ended, a slightly more composed but very pale Faye Haugen returned to the witness stand.

Questioned as to where Coreen had come from, right, left, or centre before she was struck by the vehicle, Faye could only repeat that "She wasn't there when we were going through. She wasn't!"

"She had to get off the road and then back on the road?"

"She was off the road. Everybody was off the road!"

Harry Rankin opined that Coreen had to move pretty lively to get back on the road. Sid Simons objected that Faye had not said that she saw anyone moving in a lively fashion.

"Nevertheless," interjected the coroner, "you have got her off the road and if she is coming back on, she has to move lively. . . . I don't want to get in a world's record for how fast pregnant women can run."

Rankin turned to Faye. "The truth of the matter is then, you don't know where she came from to get on that road, is that right?"

"I can't really remember."

"All you really know is that she was hit by the car on your side of the car?"

"Yes. She was on my side of the car because I remember seeing her face."

"So, you just remember the impact and you can remember her face and that is basically your total recollection of what occurred?"

"Yes."

Harry Rankin sat down.

MURRAY MILLER WANTED TO KNOW if Richard had been talking to her at the time of impact. Faye said that she had been playing with her child and had not noticed anything until she saw people on the road.

"To the best of your knowledge, did Mr. Redekop have anything, consume anything, that might in any way impair his driving in the day prior to the accident?"

"No."

"No drugs of any kind?"

"No."

As Mr. Miller sat down, the coroner had a question. "You weren't under any drugs for this tragedy to the sister of your husband? You weren't under any sedation?"

"No."

"Was he, your husband under any sedation at all? By that I mean any amphetamines or drugs that day?"

"No."

"Thank you very much for helping us," said the coroner.

At the moment of her release Faye stumbled away from the

coroner and jurors and into several pairs of comforting arms waiting for her in the front row of spectators.

The coroner turned to the jury. "Now, Mr. Foreman and Jurors, it is now 4:30 and I would ask you to go to your homes, take your ease and [I] admonish you not to talk to anyone about the evidence you have heard here, and be rude to anybody who want[s] to talk to you about it, if necessary to get them off your back. Thank you for coming here and come back at 9:30 tomorrow morning."

A COMMUNAL SIGH OF RELIEF went through the basement room of the Canadian Legion when Coroner MacDonald announced that the inquest stood adjourned until the following morning. Among the first to leave the hearing were Elder Mary John and her daughters. They had extended an open invitation to the press, to lawyers, and to any other interested parties to visit the John home on the reserve and join the family for supper. A son-in-law, George Teed, a cook of some distinction, had been at work in Mary's kitchen since early morning, preparing a meal for all comers.

"My daughter Helen and I had heard," recalls Mary John, "that reporters from the CBC, *Maclean's Magazine*, the *Globe and Mail*, and many other representatives of the news media, wanted to interview several people. We thought the meal would be a good way to get people together. On Monday night, September 27th, my family invited reporters and any other interested persons out to the reserve for dinner, served on my kitchen table. We had salads, roast moose, fried chicken, bannock, pies—you name it, we served it. But better than all the food was to see white and Native people sitting in my kitchen and living room, talking together. Many of the journalists and reporters, some of them from as far away as Toronto and Montreal, had never been on a reservation before, or eaten a meal with a Native in a Native's home.

"The chief was there, Harry Rankin, Archie Patrick, Sophie Thomas, most of the Homemakers—they were all interviewed and then the talk really began! It was a night to remember."

CHIEF TONY PRINCE, A BIG good-looking man, a carpenter by trade, had had very little to say during the weeks when Sophie Thomas and her Homemakers were pressuring the Vanderhoof coroner to hold an inquest into Coreen's death. Now at Mary John's kitchen table he was willing enough to talk about racial tension and harassment, but what really concerned him was the terrible state of living conditions on the reserve. He told Clive Cocking of the *Vancouver Sun* that transportation to town was vital for the reserve. The lack of cars in Stoney Creek village meant that people either hitch-hiked into town, which was often dangerous, or paid up to ten dollars for a taxi, which was expensive.

He worried about the housing on the reserve. Most of it, he said, was bad, and he couldn't see much chance of improvement—Ottawa only allowed $50,000 each year to build four houses. With no sewage system, he said, "a lot of people are getting sick now with kidney infection, and TB is coming back." The band had been pressing for a sewer system, but Indian Affairs didn't want to provide the money because the houses were "too spread out." "You got to go through a lot of red tape to get anything out of Ottawa," he said sadly to Clive Cocking.

IN THE LIVING ROOM OF THE John home, Harry Rankin was in a philosophical mood. Asked if he thought the inquest had shifted its emphasis from finding out how Coreen died to being a forum for Native grievances, Rankin replied, "Let me put it to you this way: I don't think life proceeds forward in a nice gentle unspoiled way. I suppose it comes as something of a surprise to this young man to find that his little case has become the centre of national importance and I suppose, to some extent, he may feel victimized. You see, what is really being looked at in the narrow sense is whether the estimates of speed of fifty and sixty and seventy miles an hour, and all the other facts, constitute the basis for laying a criminal charge."

With a pointing finger, Rankin continued, "I quite agree with you that the broader issue, which is the more important issue, is some of the social problems that arise out of this situation. I suppose it's unfortunate in life that the starting point is that a whole group of people have been getting away with something for years and somebody is caught up short and becomes a special case in that situation. But you know, that happens in real life and it can't be helped. I don't happen to think that Richard Redekop is being crucified. I happen to think that in the normal course of events an inquest should have been heard."

"But is all this fair to Richard Redekop?" asked a reporter.

"I don't know what is fair," replied Rankin. "I've lived all my life to my present age and I haven't found this a fair world. When someone says, 'Is that fair?' I just simply say I don't know. Fair to whom? Are we to be fair to an individual or fair to the whole of society? Do people get hurt in struggles? Of course they do. Is it not more fair to do some harm to an individual, if you feel he is being harmed, and try to bring some sanity to a whole society? I don't know what's fair, unless it's the larger issue that if we don't come to terms with racism, with the categorizing of some people as sub-humans, which is what racism is all about, maybe we won't survive at all. Fairness means fairness to all.

"Once you have decided that a person is sub-human, he's drunken, he's lazy, he's ignorant, he's animalish—and these are terms we've heard here and there—then the next step is the extermination question. It doesn't hurt if you boot a drunken

Indian and kill him or throw him out on his head or let him freeze outside a beer parlor at night, which has occurred on a number of occasions. So, you know, I have a sense of fairness, I think, but I also have a sense of history and a sense of a need to see things change. I simply have to say this: history or time has to judge these things."

The talk, the interviews, went on and on through the hours of darkness, there in the home of Mary and Lazare John in Stoney Creek village.

20

TWO SCHOOLS OF THOUGHT surfaced as people gathered near the entrance to the Legion Hall just after nine o'clock, Tuesday morning, September 28, 1976. On the one hand there was a prediction circulating that the inquest would run another two days. Said a spokesman for this school of thought, "Isn't it a fact that Rick Redekop is going to be called to the stand this morning, and anyone who has followed the testimony for the last three days—as I have—knows that his evidence will carry over into tomorrow?" The second estimate, put forward in the main by reporters and outside observers who had exhausted everything that Vanderhoof had to offer and wanted nothing so much as to see the hearing finished, said they had it on good authority that the inquest would wind up within a few hours.

This second forecast proved to be closer to the mark.

WITH A STANDING-ROOM-ONLY crowd before him, the coroner began proceedings by indicating that the jury wished two witnesses, Mr. Sam and Mr. Allen, to be called. Since they were not present, Coroner MacDonald said, "I think the calling of Mr. Redekop might be deferred. I myself would like to call Mayor McLeod. In the course of the last three days," explained the coroner, "I did make reference to transportation, I did make reference to the organization of the 50th Anniversary, and I did make reference to perhaps a lack of medical attention for such a celebration. I did get a message from Mayor McLeod that he wanted to see me when this was finished and I think the proper place to see me is here. So call His Worship if you would."

Mayor McLeod, a stocky rather ruddy-faced man, was duly sworn.

"Did you expect a big influx of people, and if so, were there any preparations for transportation to Stoney or elsewhere?" asked the coroner.

The mayor responded that it had never been customary to provide transportation home from social affairs. "It was never a matter considered by the committee," he said.

"Thank you," said the coroner. "That is the only question I wanted Your Worship for."

"I have a few questions, Mayor McLeod," said Harry Rankin. "I am wondering whether as between yourself and the Band you felt there would be some advantage in talking . . . every three months with the Chief and the Band and your Council to discuss general problems that may arise in the community?"

"Yes, I think so," responded the mayor. "Irregardless of accidents, I think so."

Rankin wondered about regular transportation between the town and the reserve—a pick-up truck, perhaps? The mayor thought a pick-up truck might be a bit dangerous. Rankin corrected himself. "No, I am talking about an eight passenger van. I'm sorry if I said a pick-up."

The mayor was emphatic. "I think a transportation service is certainly a desirable thing. . . . I think there is a lot of money being wasted by people who have to get taxis. . . . I think as long as those services are not there that the transportation factor is something that should be prime."

Rankin was also concerned about ambulance services. He pointed out that in the case under consideration, there appeared to be a forty minute time lapse between the call for help and the arrival of an ambulance. The mayor agreed that this service, operated by volunteers who are paid for their work, badly needed upgrading.

And the road to Stoney Creek Reserve—"I notice," said Rankin, "that in coming back and forth in the last three or four days, that it is kind of frightful. . . . Is that anything that you have any influence on as Mayor and Council?"

"We haven't any influence," replied the mayor. "I might comment," he added, "that if it is frightful now, it is certainly nothing like it would have been two or three years ago."

"Finally," said the lawyer, "another thing has occurred to me . . . as a casual observer. It is not a question of being critical—what appeared to me to be a tremendous number of young people that centre around one or two hotels. There doesn't seem to be many places or activities for them." More than this, Harry Rankin said that he noticed a number of people, obviously intoxicated, being served in the Government Liquor Store. "Has there been any direction from Council in that particular area?"

"Yes," replied the mayor. He had, he said, earlier in the year initiated a number of meetings which resulted in the RCMP detachment getting two additional officers to deal with just such problems.

"And another thing," said Rankin, "that one does observe on a Sunday here—and I have only been here the one Sunday—is the rather bad driving habits of some of your young people—well, maybe not so young . . . really what you would call a Sunday sport of using streets in a way that would be highly undesirable in a local area. . . . "

"I was driving around on Sunday," said the mayor ruefully, "so I won't comment on that."

"I didn't see you," said Rankin as he sat down.

SID SIMONS WANTED to explore the availability and cost of

using taxis, particularly when people travelled back and forth to the reserve. The answer seemed to be that the cost of a taxi was between eight and ten dollars per trip, and that this cost was often shared by several people.

"I take it your job as mayor isn't a full-time job. . . . What is your other occupation?"

"School principal [of] Vanderhoof Elementary School."

Simons elicited the information that the elementary school had an enrollment of 400 students, and that apart from some volunteer organizations mainly in the field of sports, the school system provided most of the extracurricular activities for youngsters in Vanderhoof.

Before the mayor left the witness stand, the coroner had a request to make. "I wonder," he said, "if you might not ask [the Hospital Board] if they might consider in the future having a resident living in . . . the doctor was candid enough to admit that he got a phone call and then fell back asleep again. I thought if he was asleep in the hospital the nurse could really give him a good shake and wake him up if a patient came in."

"That can be brought up," said the mayor.

The coroner turned to the foreman of the jury. "My hands are tied, Mr. Foreman, waiting for Mr. Sam and Mr. Allen—I think I am prepared to go ahead with Mr. Redekop. Call Mr. Redekop, please."

AS THE INQUEST MOVED towards its conclusion, university graduate Archie Patrick, a Carrier who was employed as a coordinator of Indian education in the school district, had some thought about placing responsibility for the plight of his people.

"I really believe," he said, "that if anyone is to be indicted, it is the Department of Indian Affairs and the media, specifically the movies. It was the movies that had the attention of the world for fifty years. . . . They portrayed an Indian as savage, someone to be feared, and a suitable candidate for shooting. This kind of idea towards Indians, and miles and miles of celluloid saying that I'm a savage, is the main crime, and we're the result of it. The fringe type in Vanderhoof would see me and recognize me as a savage and make me a worthy candidate for his wrath."

His spectacles glinting in the sun, his French-Canadian wife nearby, he continued: "This matter of harassment—I think it is something like—there's a sort of local hood element that exists in most areas—these people feel they are beyond the law and even if the law does touch them, they feel a certain thrill in going against the status quo, and in this case they prey on weak people. I suppose the Indians who drink in the local bars are the weak ones, the ones that would require sympathy, help, whatever. They view these Indians as the objects of their harassment, if you want to call it that."

But, said a Canadian Broadcasting Corporation reporter, "You do know that the people of Vanderhoof are bitter about being blamed for the actions of some of their young people?"

"I sympathize with the people of Vanderhoof," replied Patrick, "because we get the same kind of treatment. We are blamed, we are categorized, all of us, for the people who drink, who are seen on the streets. We have resented this all along, and so I think the problem has come home to roost in Vanderhoof for a time at least. Vanderhoof is no worse than other places—as a matter of fact I could name three towns that are worse. However, there is possibly one area of blame, that this situation has been in Vanderhoof all these years and the people of the village have turned a blind eye to it."

Archie Patrick had one last thing to say. "If there is any good that will come from the inquest, it would be that the people of Vanderhoof will at least begin to think they should learn a little more about the situation on Stoney Creek."

21

LOOKING NEAT IN HIS checkered shirt, good-looking, unusually pale, his face expressionless, his hair medium length and curly, Richard Redekop appeared younger than his twenty-two years. One could almost touch the tension in the Legion Hall as he moved into the witness stand.

As was the procedure with other witnesses, Cliff Macarthur read aloud Redekop's statement given to Constable Taylor at 5:15 a.m., on the morning that Coreen was killed: "Okay, I was proceeding up the hill—Stoney Creek Hill—as far as I know. There was a group of people gathered up there.

"I'm not exactly sure what the people said that were standing there, I said I was going to go down and get the police. There were some Indians yelling at me. I'm not positive or sure what they were saying. Then I turned the car around and went down and phoned the police. That was it until you picked me up."

The statement continued with Constable Taylor establishing the make of the rental car which Redekop had been driving, the fact that he and his wife had just picked up her child from the baby-sitter's home, and that at the time of the accident they were on their way to his parents' home where they were staying. In his statement, Richard Redekop thought that there were thirty people on both sides of the road. He estimated his speed at about thirty miles per hour and, in answer to the constable's question, said he had had a couple of beers earlier in the evening.

"Is that the statement you gave to Constable Taylor?" asked Macarthur.

"Yes," said Redekop.

"Would you answer Mr. Rankin's questions," requested Macarthur.

Heated words passed between Simons and Rankin as to who should commence the examination of the witness. Finally Rankin said, "I will go ahead rather than have an argument about it!"

AS HARRY RANKIN ROSE to begin his examination, there was increased stirring in the hall. In the weeks before the inquest a number of white young men and women in Vanderhoof had rallied to the support of Richard Redekop. For some he was their hero; to others he was just a good guy with whom they worked or drank or partied. When the rumour spread that he would be in the witness stand on this, the fourth day of the hearing, his supporters were at the doors of the Legion early, not only to hear his evidence, but also to show their support. One felt tension and some hostility in the hall as Rankin prepared to cross-examine.

Harry Rankin first posed the question: when, after he turned onto Stoney Creek Hill, did the witness first see people on the road?

"I seen some objects—I'm not sure—on the way up from the highway about 4th Street is where I distinguished that they were people."

"You saw them approximately two blocks away?"

"Yes, maybe."

When, asked Rankin, after the people were all over the road, did they start to move to the side?

"Well, I slowed down and as I slowed down, they spread to the side of the road," replied Redekop. He reduced his speed, he said, between 5th and 6th Streets, probably to about twenty miles per hour.

Rankin pointed to the skid marks detailed on the map close to Redekop. Yes, said the witness, those were his skid marks. "I slowed down and they [the people on the road] spread apart. I stepped on it again and regained my speed and I was carrying through—carrying on through and she [Coreen] jumped out in front."

"The whole group moved to the side of the road, including her?" asked Rankin.

"Yes. . . . I hit the brakes really hard, that I recall. I didn't slowly apply them."

Rankin turned to the speed estimate based on the skid marks arrived at by the RCMP officer. "He is saying," said Rankin, "that those skid marks indicate that at the point where they start the minimum speed was thirty-six miles per hour and that the maximum speed at that point is forty miles per hour—not saying what you were doing prior to that, mind you, at that particular point. How do you account for the differential?"

"In what way?" asked Redekop.

"Well, from what you are telling me."

Finally, after several more questions, the witness responded, "I would have to settle for what the RCMP said. I figured I was going about thirty—I don't know." He thought, he said, that the skid marks must have started very soon after he hit the brakes, and that it may have been ten or fifteen feet from there to the spot where his vehicle hit Coreen Thomas.

As Rankin questioned Redekop's estimate as to how fast she would have had to move to get from the side of the road to the point where she was struck, Sid Simons jumped to his feet. "I don't think that is a fair question to put to this witness, Your Honour!" he objected. "I am also a little concerned, Your Honour, my friend has earlier announced that he is appearing here for the Homemakers Association who have some con-cerns—specific concerns relating to specific things. It seems, with respect, that my friend is conducting a very thorough cross-examination for something that isn't related to what I understand to be his purpose in being here, but rather more a prosecutorial function and I wonder if this is really the purpose of this portion of the Hearing. We do have evidence—we have the measurements, we have the experts, and the facts will speak for themselves."

The coroner nodded.

"I know your point, Mr. Simons," he said. "I am interested too, Mr. Rankin, to see that you are more active for the Homemakers Association when you have said that you are appearing for them. You have done more on behalf of the deceased in your cross- examination—not that you haven't been helpful."

"I am here, so I might as well. . . . "

"So long as we appreciate that. I hope I haven't upset you."

Rankin grinned, his walrus moustache moving up and down. "I don't feel upset," he replied. "It takes a great deal to upset me."

The coroner nodded again. "As long as someone does it [prosecutes] and does it well, and I feel that Mr. Simons and Mr. Rankin are well qualified."

"Thank you very much, Your Honour," said Rankin. He turned to the witness. "Now, if anything I say seems unfair you correct me because I don't mean to be unfair." He continued with his previous line of questioning: the relative speed of the girl and the car just before the instant of impact. Finally the lawyer said, "She moved and then you hit your brakes. That is quick as a flash—you are young and your reactions are good?"

"Yes."

"And that is your explanation as to how the accident occurred?"

The witness agreed.

Rankin went on to ask if Richard Redekop had been paying

attention to his driving at the time of the accident. The witness affirmed that he had not been talking to Faye Haugen or playing with the baby. He added that the vehicle itself was brand new with no known malfunctions.

"Now," continued Rankin, "how many beers did you have to drink?"

"I'm not exactly sure—it could have been anywhere from four to six, I guess." He said that he had his first beer just after the dance started, close to 8:30.

"You had four to six beer and the last beer you had when?"

"I may have had a beer at the end of the street dance and I had a drink in Rotary Park."

"Does that mean hard stuff?"

"No."

"You had no hard stuff, no wine, just beer?"

"Yes."

Richard Redekop confirmed that although there may have been some marijuana smoked at the street dance, he did not smoke any. Nor did he take pills or anything else that day.

"When this woman came out in front of you, would you describe it as darting out in front of you, running, or what would your description be?"

Redekop thought it was sort of a run, but when he was asked if he would describe it as a fast or a slow run, he replied, "I don't know. While she was moving I was trying to stop, so I can't—that is what I was thinking of was stopping."

The witness said that he had been driving for six years, that he had driven the road to his parents' home many hundreds of times, that he knew the speed limit on the hill was thirty miles per hour and that lighting conditions at the time were adequate. He contradicted testimony from earlier witnesses that he had gone around a group of people before his vehicle hit Coreen. "I was continuing in a straight line up the hill," he said.

"So in summary," said Rankin, "your evidence is that you were going thirty, you see them [the crowd], you decreased to twenty, they clear off the road, and you accelerate to thirty, pass through, and this girl darts out or runs out in front of you and you apply your brakes. You weren't able to stop and you hit her?"

"Yes, I was going around thirty when it happened, yes."

"You were not able to avoid the accident because she just ran in front of you?"

"Yes, that is true."

The witness said that although he had often seen people walking and hitch-hiking on Stoney Creek Hill, the size of the crowd that morning of the accident was unusual.

"I see," said Rankin. "Thank you very much." He sat down.

AS SID SIMONS STOOD TO BEGIN his questioning, Clive Cocking of the *Vancouver Sun* was remembering Simons' comments to him about Richard Redekop. Simons had said that Richard Redekop was "no angel" and did not pretend to be. He'd been in a number of fights around town, Simons had said; he had been convicted on two minor drug charges, and was currently facing a charge of assaulting an Indian woman. But he did not deserve the kind of treatment he had been receiving. "The terrible thing is that everyone is trying to poke Ricky with all the ugliness that exists in Vanderhoof," said Simons.

Simons began with the question, "Have you ever observed a motor vehicle accident while you were at home?"

"Yes," replied Richard Redekop. "My brother was run over by a car."

"How old was your brother at the time?"

"Ten."

"Was he killed?"

"Yes, he was—not instantly."

Sid Simons moved on to the newspaper accounts covering

the death of Larry Thomas two years before, when he was struck by a car driven by Richard's brother, Stanley. "And your understanding of that particular incident was that your brother and his friends were riding in his pick-up truck and there was a man lying across the road and your brother swerved to try to avoid the person, went into the ditch, rolled over, and the occupants of the vehicle were injured as well as the man on the road?"

"That is true."

"Did each of these incidents respecting members of your family affect you in some way?"

"Yes, they did."

"Now, more recently there was an accident involving another member of your family, is that right?"

Richard Redekop confirmed that his seventeen-year-old sister was involved in a car accident just days before Coreen Thomas' death, and that in fact, she died a few hours after Coreen during the afternoon of July 3.

Simons continued, "And generally speaking how were you feeling about things during that week?"

"I wasn't feeling very good about it."

"When you were out with Faye on the evening of the street dance were you feeling in a festive or party mood?"

"No, I was not."

Redekop said that he worked with his father and brother in a logging operation near Fort St. James. He said that he often had a beer at home or stopped in at the bar after work.

"And, generally speaking, do you drink a lot more than six bottles of beer on a weekend evening?" asked Simons.

"Yes, I do."

The witness said that after the street dance, he drove to Rotary Park where he had heard a party was to be held. "It didn't seem very interesting and I stayed there for about—it could have been anywhere from one to five minutes—and then we left."

"And you met a friend there who was sipping or drinking a bottle of beer? . . . And you had a drink out of his bottle of beer, is that right?"

"Yes."

"Were you angry with anyone?"

"No."

"Were you in any way intending to be dangerous to anyone?"

"No, I wasn't."

"Were you driving in what you considered to be a safe manner?"

"Yes."

After some questions concerning the rented vehicle which Redekop had been driving, Simons asked, "Did you know Coreen Thomas prior to the accident?"

"No, I didn't."

A reporter scribbled furiously: "Redekop denies knowing Thomas—Look at notes on first day—Charlie Chaplin—Marlon Brando—paternity?"

Simons turned to the matter of the breathalyser tests.

"The police asked you for a breathalyser test. . . . Did you make any objection to that?"

"No, I just went with the officer, the smaller fellow."

The witness said that when he blew, he felt sick. Despite this he said that he blew as hard as he could. Then he added, "I sat there for a while and he [the officer] waited and did something to the machine . . . and then he said to blow again and I said 'Again?' and he said 'Yes, they have a new law that you have to blow twice.' So then I blew again."

"And the second time you blew did you blow as hard as you did the first time. . . as hard as you were able?"

"Yes."

"And did Constable Davis appear to be satisfied that you were doing your best at the time?"

"Yes."

"Were you, as you drove up Kenney Dam Road that morning, playing chicken with anyone . . . or doing anything that was intended to create a dangerous situation for somebody?"

"No, I wasn't."

"Did you feel at the time that your driving ability had been affected by what beer you had to drink that evening or morning?"

"No, I didn't."

After questioning the witness about whether or not there had been an inquest into the 1970 death of his ten-year-old brother—Richard replied that there had not—Sid Simons turned to the atmosphere between the Natives and the Redekop family after Coreen's death.

"When you were still living at your parents' home were there any other incidents following this accident? . . . Did anybody go by and shout anything at you or anything like that?"

"Yes, not exactly at me, I don't think. There was—I think it was probably to me and my brother both."

"Have you had any kind of a feud going on with the Thomas family?"

"No, I haven't."

"Did you have any reason to deliberately drive your car at Coreen Thomas?"

"No, I didn't."

"Have there been some rumours circulating that there was some reason? . . . And as a result of that were you requested to provide some blood samples?"

"Yes."

"And did you?"

"Yes."

"Thank you, Your Honour," said Simons as he sat down. "I have no further questions."

MURRAY MILLER WANTED to explore Richard Redekop's activities on the day of the street dance, particularly as those activities might have led to fatigue at the time of the accident.

"I don't recall being tired, no," replied Redekop. "It is possible but I don't recall it."

A few more questions and the evidence of Richard Redekop, for which the jury and onlookers had waited through many hours of other testimony, was finally finished.

22

AFTER THE APPEARANCE OF Richard Redekop in the witness stand, the evidence given by Vincent Sam and Bruce Allan was almost anticlimactic. As the foreman of the jury explained, it was felt that although their statements had been entered as evidence, there should be a personal examination since they seemed to be neutral witnesses.

Vincent Sam confirmed that he had not been drinking at the time of Coreen's death and that he had relatives both in the Native world of Stoney Creek and the predominantly white world of Vanderhoof—this established his sobriety and his neutrality to the satisfaction of the jurors.

"What did you tell him [the RCMP officer] as to the approximate speed of the car?" asked the foreman of the jury.

"I SAID APPROXIMATELY sixty miles per hour," replied Sam.

"Do you care to change your mind on that or . . . ?"

"No," said Sam.

Further questions followed from members of the jury. In answer to these questions, Vincent Sam insisted that the Redekop vehicle had not been going straight up the hill, as Richard Redekop had affirmed, but that it had swerved to miss one of the young men standing almost in the middle of the road.

"Mr. Sam," asked a jury member, "you know that a car that is going sixty miles an hour is going very fast. What makes you think it was going that fast?"

"It skidded quite a ways before it hit Coreen," answered Sam.

WHEN BRUCE ALLAN TOOK the witness stand, he confirmed that, like his friend Vincent Sam, he had not been drinking the night of the street dance and that he had relatives in Vanderhoof but not in Stoney Creek.

"How fast did you estimate on your evidence to the officer—how fast did you say the car was going?" asked the foreman of the jury.

"Fifty to sixty miles per hour," answered Allan.

"Do you wish to change this at all?"

"No."

"What makes you think it was going that fast?" asked a member of the jury.

"It was coming up the hill very fast."

"THAT CONCLUDES THE EVIDENCE that will be called," said Cliff MacArthur.

Just after 11:00 a.m. the coroner, his voice clear and resonant, began his address to the jury.

"Mr. Foreman and Jurors, that would appear to be all the evidence that you have in connection with the death of the deceased, Coreen Gay Thomas. This is what we call a Coroner's Act for the Province of British Columbia. It has been with us since 1848, but in fact the Coroner's system existed for perhaps three to four hundred years before. If it has one common denominator it is death, and sometimes Coroners have felt along with their juries that we speak for the dead to protect the living.

"However philosophical that may sound, you are more particularly sworn to determine when, where, how, and after what manner Coreen came to her death. You have heard all the witnesses under excellent cross-examination and examination by counsel. You have seen these exhibits and now I think you can discharge that duty that you have been sworn to do without fear, favour or affection. Just the way you have it in your mind, so you shall write it in your verdict.

"In your deliberations I would ask you to destroy all the notes you may make as you go along. I would ask that when you come back after you have delivered your verdict that you keep those conversations and discussions you have in the Jury Room silent and to yourself.

"I can't assist you any more than I have done here now except that this is an unnatural death; it must be for you to classify it either as an accident, suicide or homicide. If you find the circumstances such as in your opinion contributed to and indeed caused this fatality, you may place that in your verdict. If you find person or persons that may have caused this death then you may also put that in your verdict. The formal part of your verdict is the name of the deceased, her age, her birth, and her address. That you have. . . ."

"You will go to lunch at twelve o'clock, returning at one-thirty, but if you have a verdict before that time allow my corporal the Deputy Sheriff here to . . . [know] your wishes and they will be dealt with on that score. I will be staying in the Glen Motel if you wish me to come back and address you any further on any other point. Thank you."

WHEN THE INQUEST RESUMED at 1:30 on the afternoon of Tuesday, September 28th, feelings of suspense—what verdict would the jury bring in?—mingled with a sense of relief that soon, very soon, the hearing would be over and life would return to its usual more mundane pace.

Both sentiments proved to be slightly premature.

"Mr. Foreman and Jurors," said the coroner, "you are still under oath and although you have been charged and put in the custody of the Deputy Sheriff . . . when Crown Counsel suggested that was all the evidence I am afraid that I took the impression that it was. However, Mr. Simons under Section 23 has requested that Sergeant Dedish and Coroner Turner be called."

An exasperated sigh wafting through the audience and across the press table stirred the air as Sergeant Dedish took the witness stand.

As examined first by Cliff Macarthur, and afterwards by Sid Simons, Murray Miller, and Harry Rankin, it was established that Sergeant Dedish was the senior officer in the Vanderhoof detachment of the RCMP, that he had served in the force for twenty-one years and that he had been in charge of the detachment in Vanderhoof for three and one-half years. He was taken through the process of laying criminal charges, and stressed that although an officer in Vanderhoof could recommend, the decision as to whether or not a charge would be laid ultimately rested with the Crown Counsel's office in Prince George. "The objective of a criminal charge to be laid," said the sergeant, "is the fact that the police officer has to be satisfied in his own mind that he has sufficient evidence to prove that charge in court and the objective of it is to have a successful conviction of that charge."

Coming to the matter of the investigation into Coreen Thomas' death, Sergeant Dedish said, "I feel that was a very thorough report and investigation."

"Just briefly, Sergeant," questioned Murray Miller, "can I take it from what you said, that you don't intend to change your policy with regard to interviewing juveniles as witnesses?"

"No, I don't intend to, no."

A member of the jury wished to question the sergeant.

"Sir, you said that no charges are laid until you have a good chance to make the charges stick?"

"I didn't exactly say that. . . . The time we lay a charge ourselves or recommend a charge be laid we in our own minds feel or the investigating officer feels that he has sufficient evidence to enter a successful conviction in court," replied the sergeant.

After some discussion of the experts' estimates of speed that the Redekop vehicle had been travelling at the time of Coreen's death, the juror wondered, with the maximum figure of 47.2 and the minimum figure of 41.8, "yet you feel you didn't have a strong enough case to present a speeding charge in this case?"

"As a rule in our Department we do not prefer a speeding charge—we generally give a person a ten mile per hour leeway."

"Even in a fatality?" persisted a juror.

"No, not in a fatality. This is in regard to a speeding infraction."

"Well, we are concerned with this particular case where there was a fatality. . . ."

The sergeant's resolution was unfaltering. "I didn't feel in my own mind and after consulting with Crown Counsel that there was sufficient evidence to prefer any charge."

"That is all, thank you," said the juror.

Sergeant Dedish stepped down.

CLIFF MACARTHUR STOOD UP. "Now Mr. Simons indicated after the adjournment that he wanted Sergeant Dedish and Coroner Turner called. I was prepared to call Sergeant Dedish because I think he had some evidence which might possibly bear on the case. With respect to Coroner Turner, however, Your Honour, I feel that is getting over into quite frankly another can of worms, and we seem to have investigated or dealt with every conceivable issue in this case. For that reason I had no intention of calling Coroner Turner. However, he is available should my friend wish to call him."

"Yes, I would like to call him, Your Honour," said Sid Simons.

The coroner turned to Harry Rankin questioningly. Said Rankin, "Let's just call him, and I will agree to it to save time."

The reporters at the press table, like the people who had crowded into the Legion Hall in anticipation of the verdict, showed a bit more animation as Turner began his testimony with Sid Simons. For many of the people attending this inquest, this man had been simply a name in the newspapers and in television newscasts. Only now did he emerge as a face, a figure, a voice. For someone who remembered him as the man who said firmly, "I will never yield to political pressure," to others who thought of him as a hit- and-run motorist from the dim past, this tanned, rather brisk man was something of a disappointment.

"He's so small," whispered one woman to another.

"Shush! I want to hear what he says!" said the second woman.

Eric Turner was duly sworn.

He stated that he had been coroner in Vanderhoof since 1972 and that he was paid twenty-five dollars for an inquiry and fifty dollars for an inquest.

"So you make more if you have an inquest than if you have an inquiry?"

Turner laughed. "I don't think there is even very much pocket money involved at this time since we have to pay income tax on it!"

He stated further that he had lived in Vanderhoof for nineteen years and before that, he spent three years with the British Intelligence Corps in Burma towards the end of the war, dealing with war crimes. Prior to that, he had attended London University and then lived for five years in India where he worked in a jute mill manufacturing gunny sacks.

Questioned as to how he became coroner in Vanderhoof, he said, "Well, like many things in Vanderhoof, it started off in the coffee shop. Sergeant McLean looked at me with a speculative look in his eye and said, 'How would you like to be coroner?' and I said, 'No, thanks, find somebody else.' " Turner said that when no one else could be found, he agreed to act as coroner. He said he did point out that he had been involved in a hit and run accident some years before and the sergeant had said, "Well, that won't matter." The next thing he knew, he was notified by the Attorney General's Department that he had been appointed coroner.

Turner stated, in answer to questions on his work as coroner, that he had dealt with forty-six unnatural deaths, nine Native and thirty-seven white. As he talked in more detail about the inquiries and inquests into these deaths, particularly the inquest into the death of Larry Thomas, killed by a Redekop vehicle, and the use of a polygraph [lie detector], Harry Rankin objected. "[This] is really getting far afield." The coroner agreed.

Turning finally to the evidence presented to him in the death of Coreen Thomas, he said that after receiving reports and much personal investigation, he decided that he had all the facts, that he knew exactly where and how Coreen died, and he forwarded an Inquiry Report to the Attorney General's Department. Until he was asked by Sophie Thomas on behalf of the Homemakers to hold an inquest, he said he felt that the matter was closed. However, he told Simons, he experienced no difficulty in agreeing to an inquest.

Questioned as to strained relationships between whites and Natives, Turner said, "I think, sir, this is a case where the media has created a situation. That is a personal opinion, sir, nothing to do with my job as coroner." He said further that if he had any bias, it was a bias which operated for the benefit of the Natives.

Simons now asked, "Perhaps you would explain to us why you are not presiding at this inquest, but Mr. MacDonald had been requested to do so."

Cliff Macarthur stood up. "Your Honour, I wonder if we are

not getting a little far afield. We seem to have gone from the cause of death to an investigation of the prior coroner to investigating your appointment. I am not certain whether the jury is getting anything out of this. . . . "

"What do you think, Mr. Rankin?" asked the coroner.

"I think it is easier to let him ramble on," replied Rankin shortly.

"I don't," replied the coroner. "Frankly, I am getting fatigued."

SHORTLY AFTER RANKIN stood up to cross-examine, he read the Inquiry Report which Eric Turner sent to the Attorney General's Department in August, "The deceased was killed at 3:35 a.m. on July 3rd, 1976, as a result of being run down by a vehicle driven by Richard Brian Redekop. The deceased, in a drunken condition, darted out in front of the moving vehicle, so that collision was inevitable. No blame is attached to the driver, Redekop."

Turner admitted under cross-examination that his conclusion "no blame is attached to the driver" was not well worded. "What I really meant," he said, "was that because of the fact that no charges were being laid by the RCMP, then as far as the RCMP were concerned, he was blameless."

Why, wondered Rankin, had Turner ignored the various estimates of speed given by witnesses at the accident scene? Turner replied that for three nights he went to the same hill where Coreen had been killed and tried to estimate the speed of oncoming cars—"I [could] tell that some went faster than others, but whether the slower ones were coming at twenty miles per hour or forty miles per hour, I couldn't tell."

Tempers flared when the matter of Redekop's speed, which Coroner Turner had averaged at thirty-eight miles per hour, came up for scrutiny. Sid Simons objected to Rankin's line of questioning. "I do not think my friend should berate this witness," he said.

Rankin turned to Coroner MacDonald. "Let's get it clear whether I am berating this witness, Mr. Coroner."

"No, I do not think that you are berating the witness, you are cross-examining. . . . "

"Thank you very much," replied Rankin. "This has been one of my pleasanter trips and I wouldn't like it to change so far as Mr. Simons is concerned, endlessly interfering!"

Coroner MacDonald smiled. "I have a feeling that you two are secret friends underneath."

Rankin shrugged. "We are, but at the end of three or four days I get tired of people who are my friends."

"Well, you go on to some other subject, Mr. Rankin, or are you shortly to finish?" asked the coroner.

"I am shortly to finish, you will be pleased to know—unless someone else comes up with a couple more witnesses . . . I don't know about . . . !"

"Life is uncertain," said Sid Simons.

WHEN ERIC TURNER FINALLY stepped down, the foreman of the jury said, "If it is right and appropriate, the jury would like to recall Mr. Redekop . . . one question only."

What the jury wanted to know were details of Richard Redekop's driving record. Did he have any prior offences? As Redekop started to answer, both Simons and Macarthur rose to object. "[This] is what I am concerned about," said Macarthur, "the jury perhaps deciding the case on his previous driving record."

"I have to agree with you," said the coroner. ". . . I think we agree that he had a proper and valid driver's licence at the time . . . thank you, Mr. Redekop," he said as Redekop left the witness stand.

The coroner turned to the jury.

"Mr. Foreman and Jurors, you have already been charged. If no other person wishes to testify or ask questions, one of the questions you wanted me to advise you on was how are we going to proceed. I suggest you deliberate to five o'clock and then go home if you have not reached a verdict at that time and return at 0930 tomorrow morning and continue your deliberations. Perhaps you can let me know how you are making out through my Deputy Sheriff. . . ."

It was 3:02 p.m. when the jury retired.

Reporters, lawyers, and onlookers dispersed into little groups inside the hall or straggled out for a smoke. The last words of the coroner had an ominous ring to them; they seemed to suggest that there might be a very long wait.

23

THERE WERE HURRIED MOVEMENTS to tables and seats when the jurors filed in at 3:20 p.m., exactly eighteen minutes after they had retired to consider their verdict.

"So soon?" Elder Mary John asked her daughter.

"They must have reached their verdict when we adjourned this morning," said Helen Jones.

Of a sudden, there was a hush and the coroner spoke, his voice abnormally loud in the quiet of the hall: "Mr. Foreman, have you reached a verdict?"

"Yes, we have, Your Honour," replied Ken Luggi, foreman of the jury.

"I wonder if you would mind reading it, please," requested the coroner.

The foreman began to read in a loud clear voice, each of his words dropping like a pebble into a pool of silence. Close to the front Sophie Thomas leaned forward, a hand cupping her ear. Not far away, Richard Redekop's mother reached out to grip the hand of someone beside her.

"WE, THE JURY," READ THE FOREMAN, "having been duly empanelled, find that Coreen Gay Thomas of Stoney Creek Indian Reserve, Vanderhoof, B.C., aged twenty-one years, died on July 3rd, 1976, at approximately 3:00 a.m. as a result of intracranial hemorrhage from a fractured skull. We find that this death was unnatural and that it was accidental. We find that Richard Redekop was negligent in that the vehicle he was

194

driving was moving too fast through a crowd of people on a relatively narrow road during the hours of darkness. We recommend that:

"1. The emergency system that serves the community be upgraded so that:

"(a) the communication system notifies police, ambulance attendants, and hospital personnel as quickly as possible;

"(b) that no person be placed in the morgue before a death certificate has been issued;

"(c) that an effort be made to obtain a resident doctor for St. John Hospital.

"2. That in the case of a fatal accident where alcohol appears to be a factor, breathalyser tests be taken as soon as legally permitted and that the tests be repeated until reliable results are obtained.

"3. That RCMP officers be encouraged to have a parent or guardian present when questioning witnesses who are sixteen years or younger.

"4. That the Stoney Creek Indian Band Council and the Vanderhoof Village council work together to establish a Friendship Centre."

"Thank you, Mr. Foreman," said the coroner.

The verdict of the jurors was passed to him. As tradition demanded, the coroner said, "Mr. Foreman and Jurors, harken to your verdict as delivered by you as I shall read it." He read the verdict again. When he was finished, he turned to the jurors. "So say you all?"

"Yes," said the jurors.

"Thank you, Mr. Foreman and Jurors. I have undertaken to see that all persons that are affected are notified of the recommendations in this matter."

Coroner MacDonald turned from the jury to the people in front of him. "I would also like to thank everyone here that has participated, particularly the School Board and the School Trustees, the Legion, the caretakers here at the Legion, Coroner Eric Turner who has looked after most of these arrangements for us, the Deputy Sheriffs, our Court Reporters who assisted us, and to Crown Counsel and the other Counsel for their assistance here.

"Other than that I can only add that I hope the death of Coreen Thomas will bring a new atmosphere and a new environment and I hope that any feelings engendered here may, if not entirely dispel, certainly reduce. I think what the Mayor said—that they are going to meet—I think your recommendation in connection with the community, and indeed that a Friendship Centre or instead a Living Together Centre is what you have been after. I hope your verdict will satisfy that.

"I thank you all for your assistance."

The inquest was over.

STILL THERE WAS WORK to be done. The media people, many of them, rushed outside—there was one last picture to be taken, one last quote to be recorded before they could write "finis" to this hearing.

A tardy photographer, on the point of leaving, saw members of the Thomas family still in their seats. It took an instant to raise his camera to eye level, and that night a poignant picture appeared in newspapers across Canada. It showed the rugged features of Coreen's mother Matilda, tears streaming down her face as she clutched a weeping Margie to her. The lined face of Coreen's father was only partially visible as he looked silently at his weeping wife and daughter. Several young Indian girls stood in the background, their faces stark and sad as they offered wordless sympathy to the Thomas family.

Beyond the family group, Sophie Thomas was an aloof figure as she moved away from the Legion Hall. Days before she had let it be known that she would give no more interviews because, she had said, there were too many calls in the middle of the night and the reporters didn't print what she said in the way that she said it. Although she avoided the reporters on this Tuesday afternoon, her quiet, almost serene air seemed to say that what she had worried about in Coreen's death, the inquest jurors had worried about too.

Richard Redekop, close to his family, his arm around Faye Haugen, spoke to reporters. "I am not going to accept in my mind that I am negligent, but I guess other people will," he said slowly. "Accidental death—I believe it all the way. I believe, I know, it was an accident."

And Elder Mary John said afterwards, "I slept better that night in the belief that justice had, for once, been done."

INEVITABLY THERE WAS A REACTION to the crowds, the activity that Vanderhoof had experienced during four hectic days. The day after, with the inquest finished, the town of Vanderhoof was deserted. Motel rooms were empty except for salesmen making their regular Wednesday calls to the local stores. The bars catered only to the odd straggler—management, seeing that it was going to be that kind of a day, gave staff an unexpected day off. The coroner, the lawyers, the courtworkers and watchdogs for the RCMP and the Human Rights Commission, all, all were gone. Even the traffic on the main street seemed muted.

As if to emphasize the change, the brilliant sunshine that had replaced morning fog for four days was no more. Instead, September 29 was grey and windy, with the faintest warning in the air of the winter that would surely come. A reporter or two still lingered, hoping for a final summation of the inquest from the RCMP, the Vanderhoof coroner, or Chief Tony Prince of Stoney Creek.

One of these reporters was Clive Cocking of the *Vancouver Sun*. That day he drove out to the reserve one last time. "The wind was blowing stiff and cold, scattering brown leaves everywhere," he wrote. "At the reserve, people were making preparations for winter. At the house across from the church, a grizzled Indian in a Cowichan sweater was hammering away, fixing his roof. Down by the community hall some young Natives were working on a new house. Somewhere across the open space, in the trees, someone was chopping wood."

When Cocking tried to talk to one of the Indian women, she seemed to speak for the people of Stoney Creek, exhausted after their brief time on centre stage, when she said, "Chief says no more interviews. We just want to get back to normal."

Epilogue

"THINGS SEEMED TO GO FLAT after Richard Redekop's trial," said Elder Mary John. "For a couple of years, things jogged along as usual in Stoney creek. We worked as we had always done generation after generation. All the headlines of 1976 didn't seem to bring any changes to our village—we were still one of the poorest reserves in British Columbia. Our young people were still unemployed, our living conditions were still bad. The statements that Sophie Thomas and Archie Patrick and Kitty Bell had made to reporters in 1976 could have been made again, two years after Coreen Thomas' death."

Writing in the *Vancouver Sun* in September 1979, three years after the inquest into Coreen's death, I echoed Mary John's disenchantment. I wrote that in only one place on the reserve did I find changes: the cemetery had many new graves. "The Two Solitudes syndrome so aptly described by the media of three years ago," I concluded, "is alive and well and functioning in central British Columbia."

How were Sophie Thomas and Mary John and the rest of us—how were we to know that, in fact, a funny thing had happened on the way to the 1976 inquest? Its offshoots were so infinitely slow in coming to fruition that only years later were we able to pinpoint the events of that year as a turning point.

In fact what the 1976 inquest accomplished was to politicize the Natives of Stoney Creek; they discovered that, like the white man, they could use such institutions as the media, the various commissions, the justice system, to impact in a positive way on the world around them. And they learned as well that in the wisdom and strength of their own people lay their best hope for the future.

They had always looked to the Church, to the Department of Indian Affairs, to anything beyond themselves, to lead them out of the Slough of Despond. "All of us," said Mary John, "were having babies and raising small children and we believed we didn't have time for politics. We were still content to let the Indian Agent and the priest and the chief do our talking for us. All this changed in 1976! We discovered in that year that we could no longer knit and crochet and quilt and leave Native politics to others."

For years Sophie Thomas, like a voice in the wilderness, had been speaking out on behalf of her people. In 1976 when she went public she found that she was not alone—almost overnight her people were mobilized at her side. And when she phoned her own Native organization in Vancouver, the Homemakers, and said, "I'm in really bad trouble up here. . . . You better send someone up right away!" that mobilization became province wide.

Only later, when other crises drove the people of Stoney Creek to the edge of desperation, did the experiences of the inquest pay rich dividends. In 1978, within the space of a few weeks, the reserve lost four of its young men through drowning and other circumstances. As the village reeled under the weight of these tragedies two Natives, Archie Patrick and Helen Jones, turned to other reserves in the province and in those reserves they found the answer they were looking for—and thus the Stoney Creek Elder Society was born, dedicated to reviving Carrier culture and pride. It was a Native solution to a Native problem.

As the organization grew and as it encouraged the birth or the renewal of many other groups, it resulted in the construction

JUDGEMENT AT STONEY CREEK

of new homes and the installation of a sewage system and street lighting. Other changes came to the reserve: a small store, survival camps, the building of a potlatch complex, the teaching of the Carrier language, the revival of traditional parenting—the spinoff which resulted from the Natives of Stoney Creek taking their destiny into their own hands has really only begun. Stoney Creek Indian Reservation is not, and probably never will be, the heaven on earth we would like it to be. On the other hand, neither would its people say of it now, as one band councillor said during the inquest, "It's a real bad place to live."

Looking back one finds that many of the people whose names made headlines in 1976 and 1977—Eric Turner, Helen Jones, Coreen's mother Matilda, Cecil Raphael, Faye Haugen—are no longer alive. Death cut a wide swath through the Nechako Valley in the years after the Thomas-Redekop hearing. On the other hand many more of the main protagonists are still at centre stage: Sophie Thomas, Mary John, Harry Rankin, Peter Thomas and his daughter Margie, Murray Miller, Cliff Macarthur, A.S.K. Cook, Sid Simons, Richard Redekop, Glen MacDonald. And even now, two decades later, the name of Coreen Thomas or Richard Redekop or Eric Turner triggers a kaleidoscope of memories and we see again the high school gymnasium with mounties everywhere, and a table crowded with media people, and, out in the hall, the women of the piano fund smiling beside their freshly-brewed coffee and their trays of iced doughnuts.

THERE IS NO ANSWER to Sophie Thomas' cry, "how do you defend Coreen?" For Sophie the justice that she sought in 1976 and 1977 was just beyond her grasp. Nonetheless her efforts and the efforts of her people in those years changed life in Stoney Creek as surely as if its lazy creek suddenly ceased to flow or its gentle hillocks faded and were gone, one by one.

BRIDGET MORAN was born in Northern Ireland in 1923, and came to Success, Saskatchewan with her family as a child. In 1951, she moved to British Columbia to work as a social worker for the provincial social welfare government. From 1997 to 1989, she worked for the Prince George School District. In addition, she has worked as a freelance journalist, her work appearing on the CBC and in the *Vancouver Sun*. She retired in 1989, but not before starting her new career as a writer with the publication of *Stoney Creek Woman*, the acclaimed biography of Carrier Elder Mary John, published by Arsenal Pulp Press in 1988 and reissued in a new edition in 1997. The first edition of *Judgement at Stoney Creek* was published in 1990; her other books include *A Little Rebellion* (Arsenal, 1992), Bridget's own story about her experiences as a provincial social worker; *Justa: A First Nations Leader* (Arsenal, 1994), the biography of Carrier tribal chief Justa Monk; and *Prince George Remembered*, a self-published chapbook (1996).

In 1995, Bridget was awarded an honorary law degree from the University of Northern British Columbia in Prince George, and in 1996 received another honorary law degree from the University of Victoria. She is currently on the boards of the College of New Caledonia in Prince George and the Legal Services Society of B.C. She is also a mother of two sons and two daughters, and a grandmother as well.

Bridget continues to live in Prince George.

Victims of Benevolence ELIZABETH FURNISS The truth behind two tragedies at the Williams Lake Residential School. "A solid addition to the historical record." —*BCLA Reporter* $12.95

The Yellow Pear GU XIONG In moving words and images, artist Gu Xiong explores issues of identity and culture. "Rich in insight that allows us to see the world in a fresh light." —*Vancouver Sun* $12.95

These and other Arsenal Pulp Press titles are available at better bookstores (ask for them) or directly from the press (please add shipping charges: $3.00 for first book, $1.50 per book thereafter; Canadian residents add 7% GST):

ARSENAL PULP PRESS
103-1014 Homer Street
Vancouver, B.C. Canada V6B 2W9

Or call toll-free in North America: 1-888-600-PULP (Visa or Mastercard only).

Write or call for our free catalogue.

Check out our website at: www.arsenalpulp.com